Contents

Acknowledgements

The author is grateful to the following people for their help in putting this book together: To Mr Dick Jenkins and pupils of Cardiff High School, to Mr Mike German and pupils of Lady Mary High School, Cardiff, and to several of my own former pupils at Woodberry Down School, London.

I am especially grateful to the following teachers and pupils who, despite the pressures of coping with the first year of GCSE, gave unstinting help in supplying me with tapes, scores and annotations. With the exception of Example 7, the compositions were all performed by the pupils themselves.
Mr Robert Bunting, Advisory Teacher, Wolverhampton, and Mr David Gould, Head of Music at Smestow School, Wolverhampton, and the following pupils: Annabel Walley and Samantha Hill who composed and performed Example 6; and Elizabeth Lane (Example 10a).
Mr John Catlow, Head of Music, Camden School for Girls, and his pupils: Katya Andrusz (flute) and Jo Burkle (clarinet) (Example 8); and Fiona Parsons (singer) and Maud Hodson (piano), who together performed Maud's song (Example 10b).
Mr Jefferson Thomas, Head of Music at Rhyl High School, and Rhys Davies, the composer of Examples 7a and 7b. Rhys' pieces were performed on the tape by Mrs D. J. Thomas (flute) and Mr D. Thomas (bassoon), instrumental teachers for Clwyd County Council.
Miss Carol Garbett, Head of Music, Turnford School, Cheshunt, and the following pupils, who played their own piano pieces: Nicola Napier (Example 9a), Sally Gull (9b) and Kathryn Tinkler (9c).

I am grateful to my colleague William Salaman, who has been deeply involved in GCSE training for Music in Wales, for his helpful comments on the manuscript, and to Mr Brian Meyrick, who prepared the master tape from the pupil recordings.

The author and publishers wish to thank the following who have kindly given permission for the use of copyright material:

The Controller of Her Majesty's Stationery Office for extracts from Crown copyright material;

London and East Anglian Group, Midland Examining Group, Northern Examining Association comprised of the Associated Lancashire Schools Examining Board, Joint Matriculation Board, North Regional Examinations Board, North West Regional Examinations Board and Yorkshire & Humberside Regional Examinations Board; and the Northern Ireland Schools Examinations Council for extracts from their music syllabuses.

Every effort has been made to trace all the copyright holders but if any have been inadvertently overlooked the publishers will be pleased to make the necessary arrangement at the first opportunity.

Editors' Preface

Coursework assessment is now a central feature of GCSE. It is a major component in almost all subjects for the six Examining Groups. Its significance is made clear in the national and subject criteria, and is endorsed by the Secondary Examinations Council in its 'Working Paper 2: Coursework Assessment in GCSE'. Under the old system, coursework sometimes featured in both CSE and O level: much good and valuable work was achieved, for example, in O-level practical work and CSE mode 3 projects. However, the intentions behind the National Criteria make GCSE coursework quite different from what has gone before. Some element of coursework is now compulsory for all pupils.

CSE and O-level between them were originally designed to examine only 60% of sixteen-year-olds – at that point the least-able 40% were not to sit any examination at all. GCSE is intended to cater for all candidates and, in order to meet the needs of the whole ability range, has introduced the notion of differentiation. In principle this means that all candidates must be presented with tasks which they find manageable, satisfying and through which they can display positive achievement. Differentiated schemes of assessment are required of all subject areas – and of coursework too. That is, either the tasks set must be closely matched to learners' abilities and competences, or general tasks are set which are then differentiated by outcome – by what pupils actually do or how they perform. In practice, this combination of requirements can make coursework highly interesting and rewarding for the learner. It can also present difficulties of organisation and management for the teacher.

In many ways GCSE coursework seems more prescribed than CSE project work. The onus is now upon all teachers to structure tasks, to set and time them appropriately, and become involved in their assessment and moderation. The purpose of this series is to help teachers tackle coursework within particular subject specialisms. The National Criteria define it as comprising 'all types of activity carried out by candidates during their course of study and assessed for examination purposes'. This means that teachers need to have a clear idea of the aims and objectives of their courses, and the role that coursework tasks play in what they are trying to achieve. The way that coursework is developed within music or drama, for example, will be different from that in science or technology. It is important, too, that the National Criteria say that the 'standards applied in the assessment of coursework must always be those which apply for the final examination, irrespective of when the coursework was actually completed or the assessment made'. That is, a piece of work handed in at the beginning of the fourth year must be judged by the same standards as work completed at the end of the fifth year. It means that teachers must have a clear idea of the quality of work associated with various levels of attainment at age sixteen so that they can gauge coursework at whatever stage in the course it is completed or assessed.

This series addresses the needs of a range of subject areas. Each booklet follows a three-part structure – the first developing ideas and activities in the setting of tasks; the second consisting of a wide range of exemplars of pupils' work, and the third considering issues of assessment and moderation. Parts 1 and 3 serve to inform, raise issues and apply the more general points involved in coursework to each subject specialism. Part 2 consists of original pupil work – sometimes written, sometimes in other forms – and is used as the basis for comments in Part 3. Each author has attempted to address the many variations that still exist between Examination Boards and has attempted to take into account the needs of those teachers engaged in the production of mode 3 syllabuses.

In spite of this common format, the individual books in the series vary considerably. This is partly because the authors bring with them their own distinct perspectives and style; partly because the syllabuses across the various subject areas make very different demands on students and teachers, and partly because of the elusiveness of the term 'coursework'. The National Criteria definition is very broad and its interpretation varies considerably across Boards and subject areas. True, the coursework component is *usually* examined by the teacher and *mainly* undertaken in class, but beyond that there is little consensus as to what might constitute a coursework component.

On the whole, the books are addressed to individual teachers to help in the planning and development of their day-to-day work. However, the assessment of coursework may well depend upon the organisation of courses, and therefore be based upon group decisions or departmental organisation. We hope there is something of value here for groups and subject teams, as well as the lone class-teacher. It is important for all specialists to be aware of the work being carried out in other subject areas. As the boundaries between subjects become increasingly diffuse, we all need to be informed of developments in neighbouring subjects, and of their coursework and assessment needs.

No one can yet be an expert in GCSE coursework – at the moment we are all in the process of learning. As teachers become more practised in task-setting, recognising performance criteria, assessing coursework and undergoing moderation, the whole process will become easier and more familiar. This series is intended to ease the transition towards that stage.

Jon Nixon and Mike Watts

Introduction

The General Certificate of Secondary Education examination in Music presents a formidable challenge to teachers. Previous examinations which were generally taken by the sixteen-plus age group concentrated on only a limited range of musical expertise and experience, and were assessed by means of a limited range of examining techniques. This was particularly true of O-level. With CSE, innovatory examining methods were pioneered, such as the testing of candidates' responses to recordings taken from the repertoire. There was also a coursework element in CSE, enabling individual interests to be pursued and documented in a 'project file'. However, only a small number of pupils were ever actually entered for CSE Music, despite the fact that its target group was supposedly much larger than that for O-level. This meant that fewer children at the lower end of the measured ability range were given the opportunity to pursue Music as an examination subject, despite the fact that many so-called 'low ability' children had demonstrable musical interests and skills. It follows that many teachers now teaching GCSE will have had little experience of those aspects of CSE examining which have influenced GCSE, particularly with regard to the assessment of coursework.

However, even those teachers familiar with both O-level and CSE will find that GCSE Music contains some radical innovations. On the whole these have been welcomed by teachers and others professionally involved in Music education. It must be admitted, though, that there is a bewildering number of simultaneous innovations in the new examination, which, taken together, can seem almost overwhelmingly daunting to those faced with the taks of actually teaching the course.

All GCSE syllabuses must conform to the requirements of the National Criteria. The National Criteria consist of a series of documents produced by the government through the Secondary Examinations Council, prior to the drafting of GCSE syllabuses by the Examining Groups. Foremost among these is the *General Criteria* document, which declares the broad educational principles which are to govern the setting up of all examinations for the GCSE. Perhaps the most memorable, and most publicly known, phrase from the General Criteria is the one referring to the new examination's stress upon *positive achievement*, aiming to recognise and reward pupils for what they 'know, understand and can do', rather than penalise them for what they do not know. In addition, the General Criteria favour a move away from norm-referenced assessment, where the grades pupils achieve are the result of a statistical comparison between candidates, to criterion-referenced assessment, where grades will be rewarded in direct relationship to specified skills and achievements. The General Criteria act as a focus to enable Examining Groups to set out aims and objectives which truly reflect the nature of particular subjects. The *subject-specific* Criteria, which at the moment cover some twenty different subject areas, are a more detailed and explicit response to these general principles. Where Music is concerned, the first demand of the Criteria is that the teaching and learning activities shall themselves be truly *musical*, that is, involved with the actual sound of music and its meaning: physically, intellectually and emotionally.

All subject-specific Criteria have to spell out the main content areas or *components* of their syllabuses. For example, in French the components are: listening, reading, speaking and writing; in History they are: historical knowledge and understanding, historical enquiry and historical reasoning. The Music Criteria identify the three activities which can be truly said to form the common core of musical experience: listening, performing and composing. It is worth noticing that the gerund has been used instead of the more common form 'performance' or 'composition'. This is quite deliberate, for it focuses the emphasis on the nature of the activity, as well as on the end product. It makes us ask not only 'What does this piece of music or this performance sound like?', but also 'What aspects of musical skill, imagination and understanding are being enabled through pursuing these activities?' Following up the process whereby pupils arrive at greater musical accomplishment and deeper aural understanding will form an important part of the assessment for the GCSE. Although the Criteria name the three common core activities separately, this is simply done for clarity of presentation. Indeed some of the new options proposed for the examination fall into more than one category. Improvisation, for example, involves elements of both performing and composing. In many musical encounters, all three activities may be subtly interwoven. Listening, above all, is an integral and inextricable element of both the other components.

Listening also exists as an 'activity' in its own right, divorced from the making of music. This aspect is covered in the final timed written paper recommended by the Criteria for all Boards to set and mark externally. Here, candidates will be required to give brief written responses to extracts heard on tape. As the teacher plays no part in the final assessment of this part of the examination, discussion of listening as a separate component is outside the scope of this booklet. But the development of the ability to listen to the sound of one's own performing, either as a soloist or in combination with others, or to listen to and to remember the sounds heard in the mind's imagination when composing is, of course, crucial to the success of both these activities. Teachers will need to plan lessons so that the three components are not always perceived as completely unrelated. Listening to music from the repertory, if carefully chosen and timed, can act as a vital stimulus to music-making.

Performing, not universally compulsory for either O-level or CSE, will form a major part of the new examination. The Criteria allow scope for both internal and external assessment of performing. Internal assessments of performing should in any case be undertaken periodically by teachers, whatever form the final assessment may take. Some Boards require that the final assessment be made by the teacher, but recorded on tape for moderation purposes. Other Boards require the assessment to be made by the teacher in collaboration with a visiting examiner, who acts as Moderator. Or, as is the case with three of the Examining Groups, the final performing assessment may be conducted entirely by an external examiner. This booklet is concerned with performing as coursework, that is, where the teacher plays a major role in the final assessment.

The most far-reaching change wrought by the advent of the GCSE is in the emphasis placed upon the third component, composing. There will be no final timed test in this component, and assessment will consist entirely of coursework. Relatively modest composing activities such as melody writing and harmonisation have long featured in O-level and CSE. The GCSE Criteria, however, envisage a much wider range of composing activities, using a variety of instrumental and vocal media, styles and forms.

This booklet aims to help teachers come to terms with the complex demands of Music coursework. Composing will receive special emphasis as both the nature of the activity, and the fact that it is a coursework component, open up uncharted territory for many teachers. Performing as a coursework activity will also be covered, and the primacy of listening in all musical pursuits, active or passive, will be stressed throughout. There will be a description of the range of activities available, an account of the forms of monitoring and documentation that are special to Music, and advice about ways of presenting these for external scrutiny.

The booklet is in three parts. Part 1 introduces the reader to what is new in content and structure of the GCSE, and makes suggestions about organisation, and the initiation of practical tasks. Part 2 consists of examples of pupils' work, all of which can be heard on the tape which accompanies this booklet, the scores of some being reproduced in facsimile in the text. Frequent reference to these is made in Parts 1 and 3, and several form the basis for Activities. When the word 'Example' appears, with an upper-case initial, it should be taken to refer specifically to the tape and manuscript illustrations that form Part 2. Part 3 considers assessment and its communication in a helpful and unambiguous form to both pupils and parents, together with issues such as moderation and grading.

A number of *Activities* appear throughout the book, and the reader is invited to participate in them. Some require the investigation and/or verification of factual aspects of the GCSE requirements. Others invite the reader to listen to and study the Examples in Part 2. The aim of the Activities is to help the teacher come to terms with the wide range of music-making styles in which young people are interested today and to consider his or her own situation in school in relation to the GCSE. Teachers who are working to a syllabus where only composing is assessed as coursework may wish to omit the sections on performing, although these may be found to contain information useful to all teachers, whether or not their pupils' performing is assessed internally.

PART 1 Task setting

1 Coursework defined

Any activity assessed by the teacher for examination purposes counts as coursework. The National Criteria for Music require composing to be a coursework activity in all syllabuses. With performing, the Criteria allow the Examining Groups a choice between internal and external assessment. With three of the six Groups, performing is assessed by a visiting examiner, with two, performing forms part of coursework, and the remaining Group, the Southern Examining Group, combines internal and external assessment in the final examination. Listening, taken as a separate component, will be assessed by means of a test set and marked externally. Although this means that its separate assessment will not feature as part of coursework, listening has an invaluable role if it is effectively integrated with practical work throughout the course, providing both models and support for performing and composing projects undertaken.

Some kinds of coursework which were acceptable for CSE will no longer be valid for presentation. Written essay-type projects, for example, will not be allowed. Some teachers may feel concerned that pupils continuing to A-level and academic musical studies beyond will have lacked experience of quasi-musicological investigative work. Experience has shown, however, that a great majority of pupils studying Music in the 14–16 age-group will not have acquired sufficient grounding in the repertoire *as listeners* to enable them to undertake such investigations profitably. The writer's own experience of several years of marking O-level essays and CSE projects has persuaded him that much of this work lacked conviction, and was derived heavily from books and other written sources rather than from pupils' direct contact with the music being 'studied'. With the Criteria's intention that Music syllabuses should give pupils first-hand encounters with music in all three components of the course, and 'hands on' experience in two of them, there is good reason to suppose that the GCSE may actually provide a better support for later musicological study than some of the practices accepted in the past as valid for O-level. Extended essays may not feature in Music coursework, but pupils will get plenty of practice writing them in coursework for other subjects. The writing of well-argued prose is a skill essential for a historian, but it is not essential for a musician. For teachers unhappy about this radical change in academic emphasis, there is at least one syllabus in the 'History and Appreciation of Music' administered by the Northern Examining Association (NEA), which may be studied as an alternative to that Board's syllabus entitled simply 'Music'. Another coursework activity which featured frequently in the CSE, the making of an instrument, will also no longer be allowable, for the skills demonstrated are those of Craft, Design and Technology, a subject area where they will doubtless find a place.

Coursework for the GCSE will therefore be entirely concerned with the *making* of music. Coursework in performing will, in general, be the recreation of music composed by others. The pupil will perform as an individual, as a member of a group or, on occasion, as the director of a group. Monitoring will be by means of tape-recording for assessment and moderation purposes. Coursework in composing will be the origination of music by the pupil. It will be acceptable for a completed composition to be presented simply in the form of a notated score. However, it is to be hoped that teachers and pupils will take the opportunity to make compositions come alive in sound by means of performance wherever possible. Scores and tape-recordings will be the means for preserving composing coursework in a permanent form for assessment and moderation.

In many 'academic' subjects, the term 'coursework' carries the implication that it is work done in the candidate's own time, free of pressure to prepare for timed assessment occasions. In Music, this certainly applies where composing is concerned, and the activity will benefit from being relieved of the stress that attended old-style written examinations. After all, which professional composers have ever produced anything worthwhile beavering away in silence in a hall filled with other people? However, a rather different argument applies to performing, an important aspect of which is the pressure to prepare for an occasion. Performing is by its nature an activity which occupies a specified time. A formal 'test' of performance does, to a certain extent, reflect the reality of music-making. It is, after all, nothing other than a recital to an audience. For many pupils, the pressure to prepare for such occasions may be beneficial, with the adrenalin generated serving to heighten the ability to communicate musically. So tests of performing run to a specified format will form part of GCSE Music. When all such tests are conducted with the candidate's teacher as the only assessor present, then performing is defined as a coursework activity, although the final assessment session will need to be taped for purposes of moderation. The main benefit of performing as coursework is that the teacher will be in a position not only to assess the end-recital, but will be able to relate it to the practice and rehearsal that led up to the occasion.

The National Criteria allow for the following range of choices in constructing mark weightings for a syllabus:

A	B	C	
Listening	Performing	Composing	to a maximum of 100 marks
25–40	25–40	25–40	

The following table gives the weightings for the different Group syllabuses:

Group	*Listening*	*Performing*	*Composing*
LEAG	38	32	30*
SEG	40	30†	30*
MEG (A)	40	30	30*
MEG (B)	25	35* or 40*	35* or 40*
NEA	40	30*	30*
WJEC	40	30	30*
NISEC	40	35	25*

*denotes a component which is coursework
†denotes a component combining internal and external assessment

There are considerable differences, not only in the weightings attached to individual components of each syllabus, but also in the importance given to coursework. The Northern Ireland (NISEC) syllabus is the one most cautious of innovation on both counts, attaching the minimum weighting to composing, and making it the only coursework requirement of the syllabus. At the other extreme, the Midland (MEG) 'B' syllabus gives the lowest weighting to the listening paper, and allows flexibility to teachers and their pupils by giving a choice of weightings for performing and for composing. A maximum of only

25% of the marks can be awarded for coursework under the NISEC syllabus, contrasted with 75% in the case of MEG (B).

These weightings will have to be carefully considered by the teacher when planning the distribution of teaching over the course as a whole. Coursework submissions for moderation will probably need to be submitted by the end of the spring term of the second year of the course, leaving the final summer term free for intensive preparation for the timed written listening paper, and for the practical performing tests, if they are to be conducted by an outside examiner. There are, therefore, probably only five terms in which to complete coursework assignments.

It is reasonable to assume that, despite any other positive response to a call for greater resources to support the teaching of the new syllabuses, there is unlikely to be any increase in the number of periods made available for Music at fourth and fifth year level. In comparison with other subjects, Music in most schools does enjoy an extra resource in the form of instrumental tuition, and it would be foolish not to make full use of this in the service of the performing component, even to the extent of involving peripatetic staff in the assessment process.

It is assumed that a normal timetable allocation for GCSE Music will be the same as for O-level or CSE, that is, generally two double periods per week, a normal period lasting about 35 minutes. This gives 140 minutes per week. The following table suggests a breakdown for the allocation of the three components for a 'normal' teaching week:

First double period:	Listening	25 minutes
	Performing	45 minutes
Second double period:	Composing	55 minutes
	Listening	15 minutes

Although most syllabuses give listening a greater mark weighting, it takes less time to organise within a lesson than practical work. Composing, on the other hand, and especially *individual* rather than group composing, will be a relatively new activity for both pupils and their teachers. It does not, on the whole, enjoy the support of outside tuition in the way that performing does, and will therefore need more classroom time to get it going.

Another overall approach to planning the course might be to devise a modular structure, working in half-term units, concentrating in turn on each of the three areas. However, this may lead to an undesirable compartmentalisation of the three components, which, ideally, should be integrated. However, it is acknowledged that both composing and performing would benefit from the more intensive focus that a modular approach can give. A compromise might be to keep all three elements going, but to give heightened prominence to one of the two practical elements over a half-term period. So a half-term emphasising the performing side would organise the week's teaching as follows:

First double period:	Performing	70 minutes
Second double period:	Composing	35 minutes
	Listening	35 minutes

Such an arrangement might be helpful at the start of the two-year course, with composing being introduced more gently, and in shorter sessions, the 'ice being broken' through the more familiar activity of performing. After the half-term break, composing would then be given the double period, with the remaining time being shared between listening and performing. The listening element will benefit from both composing and performing being coursework activities, if, as expected, all submissions for moderation have to be in by spring of the second year of the course. The entire teaching time of the final summer term can then be used to prepare for the listening paper.

Clear thinking is needed to enable the teacher to plan a week's work for the GCSE class. Decisions have to be made as to which activities should be planned for the classroom, and pupils will need guidance in planning work to be pursued in their own time. Much performing may receive substantial stimulus and support from instrumental teachers, so performing in the classroom must not simply duplicate this, but aim at extending and complementing it. In particular, the opportunities for ensemble performing that the classroom offers should be taken up and explored. (Hear, for instance, Example 2b, 'Dido's Lament'.) As with all subjects being studied for the examination, a large amount of work will need to be done by the pupil outside lesson times. This means both individual study for homework, and, in the case of Music, involvement in extra-curricular ensemble activities, which should be regarded as an essential part of the course. There follows a summary of the activities a pupil will need to pursue in order to support and develop work initiated in the classroom lesson.

Listening

Pupils will need to listen widely as part of their homework in order to prepare for the varied repertoire contained in the final timed written paper. These days, there is plenty of access to recorded music in all styles, and both radio and television provide a rich and varied source of listening material. The teacher should supplement the pupils' home listening with opportunities to hear music performed live, organising trips to concerts, shows, etc.

Listening is the crucial integrating factor in Music GCSE. It should be pursued as an activity related to and not separated from the other two components.

Performing

Pupils will need to practise their performing skills, supported where possible by instrumental lessons. Both individual practice and group activities should be organised to continue outside lesson times to enable the pupils' skills to develop to their full potential.

Composing

Merely composing during lesson time will be far from sufficient. Lessons should be a time for initiating, trying out and consolidating ideas, as well as assessing them. Real composing work will have to be done at home, if at all possible. (This assumes that a keyboard or some other sound source can be made available at home to enable ideas to be tried out.) If composing cannot be done at home, time, space and resources will need to be made available at school, in conditions where a pupil can hear and test ideas at leisure, without the pressure of a time limit or excessive competing noise from other pupils.

Even given this range of outside practice, participation and individual study, the GCSE teacher will still feel under pressure to complete the course within five terms, using only the limited amount of time available for lessons. Apart from instrumental tuition, it is important also to make available to pupils other activities which may stimulate, strengthen and consolidate work for the GCSE.

Teachers should be on the look-out for day or weekend courses in performing or composing: youth orchestra courses held at weekends or half-terms, courses for jazz bands, rock groups or in the use of modern digital technology, all of which can be very stimulating and add enrichment to pupils' studies for the GCSE.

Activity 1 ***Background reading***

Teachers involved in organising courses for Music GCSE will find it useful to read all or some of the following:

1. *GCSE: The General Criteria* (DES)
2. *The National Criteria for Music* (DES)
3. *Music GCSE – a Guide for Teachers* (SEC and OU)
4. *Working Paper 1 – Differentiated Assessment in GCSE* (SEC)
5. *Working Paper 2 – Coursework Assessment in GCSE* (SEC)
6. GCSE Music syllabuses, and past or specimen papers
7. *Music from 5 to 16, Curriculum Matters 4* (DES)

---

2 Performing

What is performing for GCSE?

The performing examination will fall into two sections: *prepared performance* and *unprepared performance*. In the prepared performance section, all syllabuses follow the Criteria's requirement that candidates shall opt for *two* out of the following:

3.2.1 Singing or playing individually
3.2.2 Singing or playing in an ensemble
3.2.3 Rehearsing and directing an ensemble

The Criteria also require candidates to offer *two* of the following options for unprepared performance:

3.2.4 Performance of previously unseen music
3.2.5 Repetition of musical phrases given aurally
3.2.6 Improvisation

Nearly all syllabuses adhere to the Criteria requirements for unprepared performance, but there are two exceptions. The Welsh Joint Education Committee (WJEC) require all candidates to take a sight-singing (or sight-whistling) test in addition to the two chosen options, and the Midland Examining Group's 'A' syllabus makes the repetition of phrases given aurally compulsory, while allowing a choice between improvisation or sight-reading.

How much performing work has to be done?

The following table summarises the quantity and duration of the performing assessment requirements for the different Examining Groups.

PREPARED PERFORMANCE		
Option	*No. of pieces*	*Duration*
Individual performance		
LEAG	One or two	5 minutes
SEG	At least one	Not specified
MEG (A)	One or two	5 minutes
MEG (B)	One or two[1]	5–10 minutes
NEA	Two	Not specified
WJEC	Not specified	5 minutes
NISEC	One or two	5 minutes
Ensemble performance		
LEAG	One or two	5 minutes
SEG	At least one	Not specified
MEG (A)	One or two	5 minutes
MEG (B)	One or two[1]	5–10 minutes
NEA	Two	Not specified
WJEC	Not specified	Not specified
NISEC	One or two	5 minutes

Rehearsing and directing		
LEAG	One or more	5 minutes
SEG	Not specified	10–20 minutes
MEG (A)	One or two	5–10 minutes
MEG (B)	One or two[1]	5–10 minutes
NEA	Two[2]	Not specified
WJEC	Not specified	10 minutes
NISEC	One	10–15 minutes

Notes
(1) The MEG (B) syllabus stipulates a total of THREE pieces over the two options chosen, with the prepared performing assessment session lasting about fifteen minutes.
(2) The NEA requires, in addition to the final rehearsal session, a written and/or taped record of rehearsal progress of the pieces over a period of time.

The following table gives the requirements for unprepared performance. This session is unlikely to take more than 10–15 minutes, so the third column gives the amount of preparation time allowed for each option. Where sight-reading is concerned, the preparation will normally take place immediately before the test. The improvisation option is generally allowed a longer period for preparation, of up to fifteen minutes.

UNPREPARED PERFORMANCE		
Option	*No. of pieces*	*Preparation*
Performance of previously unseen music		
LEAG	Four stepped tests[1]	30 seconds
SEG	Three stepped tests	Not specified
MEG (A)	Three stepped tests	10 minutes
MEG (B)	Two stepped tests	1 minute
NEA	Two stepped tests	1 minute each
WJEC	Three stepped tests[2]	Not specified
NISEC	Three stepped tests	10 minutes
Repetition of musical phrases given aurally[3]		
LEAG	Four stepped tests	
SEG	Three stepped tests	
MEG (A)	One test	
MEG (B)	Two stepped tests	
NEA	Two stepped tests	
WJEC	Three stepped tests	
NISEC	Four stepped tests	
Improvisation[4]		
LEAG	Two pieces	15 minutes
SEG	One piece	10 minutes
MEG (A)	One piece	10 minutes
MEG (B)	One piece	15 minutes
NEA	One piece	5 minutes
WJEC	One piece	10 minutes
NISEC	One or two pieces[5]	10 minutes

Notes
(1) 'Stepped' tests are tests graded in order of increasing difficulty.
(2) The WJEC includes a compulsory sight-singing test.
(3) No preparation time is required for this option.
(4) All Examining Groups offer a choice of stimulus for improvisation.
(5) The second piece, a more ambitious improvisation challenge, is not compulsory.

To sum up, most performing assessment sessions should last not longer than about half an hour, with not more than two pieces being offered in each of the prepared performance options. Where performing is part of coursework, arrangements for internal assessment can be more informal, spread over a fairly long period of time, and incorporated into the normal performing activities of a music lesson.

In what way does it differ from O-level or CSE?

There are three important ways in which performing for GCSE is different:

- Performing will be compulsory for all candidates. It was not universally compulsory for either CSE or O-level.
- The form of the practical examination determined by each individual syllabus must conform to the requirements of the Criteria (see above). The use of graded examinations of outside agencies such as the local examination boards as a means of qualification for, or exemption from, the 'performing' component will no longer be allowed.
- The assessment of performing may be internal or external, as explained in Chapter 1. Both kinds of assessment will be subject to moderation.

These three factors combined give performing a much higher profile in the GCSE than it had in either O-level or CSE. It means that performing can now be central to, rather than on the periphery of, classroom activities undertaken during the course. There can be continuity between active music-making in lessons in years 1–3 (ages 11–14) and work for the new examination. Such continuity was often lost in the transition to O-level, and was a cause of disillusion for many pupils. A new partnership can now be forged between class music teachers and instrumental teachers so that they, too, can become directly involved in preparing pupils for GCSE.

What kind of tasks should be set for the performing component?

It seems that performing work for GCSE will fall into the following categories:

- performing initiated by the GCSE class teacher;
- performing initiated by the pupil's instrumental (or singing) teacher;
- performing initiated by the pupil.

Performing initiated by the GCSE class teacher

It is the class teacher who is ultimately responsible for deciding the pattern of the pupil's contribution to the performing component. Where pupils are undergoing instrumental tuition, the teacher will need to liase with instrumental teachers on choice of repertoire. Instrumental teachers will need to understand clearly that they now have a role in preparing pupils for the GCSE. GCSE class teachers may wish to encourage instrumental teachers to be involved in other ways, such as organising or writing arrangements for ensemble groups to perform in the examination, or tutoring pupils for the unprepared performing tasks.

The class teacher will be responsible for organising periodic performing assessments. The simplest way to do this is to hold sessions during a timetabled GCSE period, with all the other members of the class present to hear one another's performing. It seems strange that, in an art intended to communicate with an audience, so many pupils seem reluctant to perform to one another. One of the extra-musical aims of the GCSE course should be for the teacher to work towards trying to overcome this reluctance.

It is most likely that the GCSE teacher will be responsible for organising the group performance option, either initiating groups within the GCSE class, or facilitating liaison between pupils and outside groups to which they may belong. The former may involve dealing with a heterogeneous collection of skills and instruments (see Example 2b, 'Dido's Lament'). The teacher's own skill as arranger may well be in demand for ensemble performance activities, especially in view of the requirement that no part be doubled.

Performing initiated by the pupil's instrumental (or singing) teacher

Instrumental teachers will have a crucial role to play in helping to prepare those of their pupils who are being entered for the GCSE. Advice in the selection of the best possible repertoire to perform will be one of their most important tasks. The idea that it is they, and not the Examining Board for GCSE, who select the pieces may take some getting used to. Although the repertoire prescribed for grade examinations is perfectly suitable for using again for assessment at GCSE level, it is to be hoped that teachers will take the opportunity to show a little adventurousness and explore the vast repertoire outside that of the grade examinations. Although most instrumental teachers will be quite happy to take on board the preparation of the echo-work and sight-reading options for unprepared performance, many may be reluctant to tackle improvisation as an option. However, instrumental teachers have many and varying skills, and the GCSE may reveal unexpected teaching talents among peripatetic staff, just as it will certainly reveal unexpected musical talents among pupils. Instrumental teachers may show a penchant for getting together and arranging for the kind of small ensemble that is ideal for GCSE work, and will certainly be able to advise on ensemble repertoire if the GCSE teacher's knowledge is lacking in this area.

Performing initiated by the pupils themselves

Pupils, too, will be free to choose what to perform. Some pupils will bring to the GCSE class a definite idea of what they want to do, and an established repertoire to perform. Such is the case with many folk and rock performers (Example 2c).

However, the teacher does have a role to play in encouraging the work of such pupils, giving them challenges that they might not have met before, and encouraging those of disparate musical interests to perform together (Example 2b). There will be a much wider range of skills and abilities than were measured at either O-level or CSE. Candidates may range from instrumentalists of Grade VI standard and above, to those whose only performing skill consists of being able to sing popular songs from the charts. Many pupils of low measured academic ability do the latter very well indeed, and are able to observe performance detail, sing in tune and keep time.

In what way does performing assessment for GCSE compare with grade examinations?

The grade examinations of local agencies such as the Associated Board of the Royal Schools of Music have had a long and useful history. They do not, however, offer assessment for a complete range of instruments, nor do they allow scope for candidates with performing skills outside the classical repertoire who are unable to read staff notation. The grade examining boards prescribe set pieces for their performing examinations.

In the GCSE, there will be no limitations as to choice of instrument or musical style. There will be no set pieces to perform – the choice of repertoire will be a matter of negotiation between pupil and teacher. Nor is it a requirement that notation be used, either as a means of learning a piece or as an aid to performing it. Therefore, the candidate who performs 'by ear', and many 'non-classical' styles are picked up in this way, should not be disadvantaged in this area of the examination.

Two aspects of the unprepared performing work for GCSE are similar to the requirements of grade examinations: sight-reading and echo-work (the repetition of phrases given aurally). The main difference is that, in general, they will be a part of an option scheme rather than compulsory.

The procedure followed in reporting the results by some local examination boards is an admirable example of helpful feedback. The dual description succinctly conveyed by an expression such as 'Merit (120+ marks) in Grade V' is easily understood by both pupils and parents. The *mark* indicates musical attainment, and the grade gives the level of difficulty of the tasks involved.

GCSE has also addressed itself to marking procedures that take both these factors into account. But whereas the level of difficulty of grade examinations is pre-determined by the prescribed pieces, the wide choice open to GCSE candidates will mean that both attainment *and* the level of difficulty will be variables for GCSE. (See Part 3, Chapter 2.)

A grade examiner also writes an appraisal on the candidate's mark sheet. This can give a constructive profile of attainment in all sections of the examination, and indeed makes most one-line school subject reports, or the baldly stated letter-grades on O-level and CSE certificates, seem scant and unhelpful by comparison.

Grade examinations are musically conservative in many ways, yet educationists outside music have admired and sought to emulate their tradition of criterion-referenced assessment and detailed reporting of results. The influence of music grade examinations has been evident in the recent development of graded objectives in modern languages, for example.

Activity 2 Planning your individual performing programme

With a list of your fourth year GCSE pupils handy, list the individual performing activities of which they are capable. Pay attention to the following points:

1 What help and support can you count on from your instrumental teaching colleagues?
2 Are there pupils who will depend entirely on your own help to see them through?
3 At the other extreme, are there pupils who have developed musical skills quite independently of 'teaching' in the conventional sense?
4 What individual performing activity will the candidate be best assessed in? A few candidates may have more than one performing skill – for example, a singer may be an instrumentalist, or may be accomplished in more than one performing style; a classically trained trombonist may also play jazz, and so on. No credit is given for having more than one individual performing skill, but versatility may well add to the interest and enjoyment of the course.
5 Do the candidates have a performing repertoire – are there individual pieces they can already perform reasonably competently? Are they literally solos, or will they require accompaniment?

Are there any performing activities not eligible for assessment in the GCSE?

The initial impression given by the wide musical canvas of the GCSE might be that an unlimited range of performing opportunities was available for assessment. However, there are one or two kinds of performing which will not be allowed.

GCSE assessment must focus upon individual attainment. The Criteria explicitly require that:

> 4.2.3 The candidate's part must not be doubled in any other part of the ensemble.

Corporate musical activities, such as choral singing or playing in a string section of an orchestra, are among the most valuable experiences music education can offer. But they cannot be fairly assessed as the candidate's own work, as the individual contribution is not readily identifiable. In the past, some CSE boards made a requirement that candidates produce evidence that they had taken part in an ensemble, and choirs and orchestras were included in the definition of an ensemble for this purpose. In the GCSE, all activities counting towards the award of a certificate must be identifiable and assessable.

What constitutes an 'ensemble'?

The Criteria stipulate that:

> 4.2.4 A candidate may meet the requirements for individual performance (3.2.1) and performance in an ensemble (3.2.2) by presenting two suitable accompanied performances.

So pieces involving two performers, such as an accompanied 'cello piece (Example 1d), or a drummer playing alongside a pianist (Example 2c), are eligible for assessment in either option. The criterion for successful participation in an ensemble is the meeting of musical minds; that is, the candidate's ability to listen to, and blend in with, at least one other performer. A self-accompanied performance, such as a singer playing guitar or piano, would not, therefore, qualify as an ensemble. The Northern Examining Association is more stringent than the Criteria in this respect, for it stipulates that an ensemble comprise no fewer than three performers. All other syllabuses allow an accompanied solo performance to qualify as an ensemble.

What is involved in rehearsing and directing an ensemble?

This, the third option in the prepared performing section, offers an interesting opportunity for candidates who show inclination and talent for the running of musical groups. The wording of the Criteria allows scope for interpretation. The term 'rehearsing and directing', generally understood to mean 'conducting', can mean other things as well. Many jazz groups, for example, are led by participant-performers directing from their own instruments, in the manner of eighteenth century Cantors and Kappelmeisters. Recording producers working with rock musicians, building up tracks in layers for a final mix for the master tape, are also involved in rehearsing and directing, fine-tuning a performance in aspects such as balance and intonation. Given the growth of good recording equipment in schools, one or two pupils with an interest in recording production may well emerge in GCSE classes from time to time. A session where a pupil is constructively engaged in getting the best possible performance from a group prior to taping them could certainly be assessed under this option.

The 'rehearsing and directing' option by its nature focuses the attention onto the *process* of making music, for it is only by hearing the way a director is able to break down a performance into rehearsable components, and deal with these clearly, decisively and artistically, that an assessment can be made. One examining group, the NEA, requires an account to be kept of the development of the ensemble under the candidate's direction in the form of a written and/or taped record of rehearsal progress. But the assessment of *process* should play a part in all aspects of GCSE music, and not just in cases where the nature of the activity compels a focus on it.

Activity 3 Planning ensemble performance activities

All members of your GCSE group will have to be involved in ensemble work during the course, either as members of a performing group, or as directors. Are there any 'natural' ensembles already within your GCSE class? Do they themselves have a clear idea of the kind of music they wish to perform as a group (as a pop group/reggae band might), or will you have to initiate their group performing activities, even writing/making arrangements yourself?

Are your ensembles such that individual performers will be clearly audible? Are there any natural leaders, musically speaking, among your GCSE class who might be able to take the rehearsing and directing option?

Remember: all syllabuses (except NEA) allow an ensemble of a minimum of two players, so an accompanied solo performance can count as an ensemble.

Some of your pupils may belong to ensembles with performers who are not members of your GCSE group. If these pupils wish to enter performance in their 'outside' ensemble for GCSE, will you be able to organise an assessment? For example, one of your pupils may play in a local band, organised and run through the adult education network. Will you be able to liaise with the tutor running the ensemble to arrange an assessment and possibly make a tape recording?

Will candidates need to be able to read music in order to perform?

Apart from the WJEC's sight-singing requirement, there is no stipulation that candidates will need to be able to read staff notation in order to qualify for the performing component. In the introduction to the Criteria, it is stressed that a GCSE syllabus must:

> 1.2.2 admit those areas of musical experience in which pupils demonstrate keen interest and skill.

Belated recognition is now being given to the fact that western 'classical' music with its associated system of staff notation is not the only area where young people at school can show musical skill. It must be remembered that what children know, understand and can do is not necessarily exclusively the same as what they have been taught. The GCSE allows for expertise gained outside school to be recognised and developed. This is particularly the case with children from those communities, including ethnic minorities, that have highly developed musical cultures of their own. These cultures may have musical values that differ in important ways from those implied in the O-level examination, with its exclusive concentration on the study of western classical music. Many non-classical styles of performing are picked up by ear, and their absorption into the musical bloodstream is no less thorough than that of notated styles. Indeed in many instances, the direct contact with sound afforded by learning from recordings or live performances rather than from dots enables many musically aware youngsters to observe subtle features not readily conveyed by notation. Examples of these would be 'blue notes' in rock or jazz music, and certain characteristic kinds of articulation or vibrato. (Hear Examples 2c and 3a–d.)

This is not to downgrade the value of learning to read music, but the importance of notation needs to be seen in perspective once we accept the need for an examination that admits a wider range of skills and enthusiasms. Besides, staff notation is not the only form of notation. Steel bands may opt to play from their own special tablature, jazz musicians will read from a combination of chord symbols and staff notation, Baroque continuo players will read and improvise from a figured bass, and those performers who have picked up their skills entirely aurally, as is the case with many folk and rock performers, will make their sounds without reference to any form of written or printed code.

Nor should it be forgotten that the performance of classical music is also handed down by ear – dots on paper alone cannot convey ornamentation and other subtleties. These can only be transmitted by personal contact with musicians from previous generations, or through recordings. Imagine, for example, a pianist who had never heard a stylish performance of the piece trying to cope with the complex and rhythmically elusive figurations in Chopin's F sharp minor prelude!

Fluency in staff notation is needed for 'classical' performing, but where many other styles are concerned it is not a requirement either for individual or for ensemble work. Also, if we take the term 'rehearsing and directing' as being open to wider interpretation than simply meaning 'conducting' in the conventional sense, it is not always essential for this option either.

Where unprepared performance is concerned, the Criteria have again been at pains to allow both literate and non-literate musicians opportunities to demonstrate their competence. There is a choice of two out of three options: sight-reading, echo-work and improvisation, allowing for a divergence of skills.

There has been a less than wholehearted response from some of the Examining Groups to the Criteria's demand for openness to pupils lacking a background in conventional music-reading. The WJEC's compulsory sight-singing test has been mentioned already. The LEAG requires that 'a copy of the score (or a commentary where no score is available) must be supplied for the examiner's use during the prepared performance assessment'.

The SEG syllabus (p. 5) even raises the possibility that music which does not exist in a notated form may create problems of comprehension for examiners, although it is difficult to see how a score, or other means of explanatory support, necessarily makes a piece easier to understand!

Although annotations have their value in indicating the learning processes involved, it is to be hoped that later versions of syllabuses will have the confidence to dispense with requirements such as verbal 'programme notes', once teachers and examiners in Music are more used to encouraging and appraising the work of a wider range of pupils. There seems to be a traditional reluctance in music education, and indeed in music generally, if one goes by the verbiage that is produced to go with records, concerts and broadcasts, to allow sounds to speak for themselves. Although different cultures may emphasise different aspects of sound and performing style, it is the similarities between disparate musics that matter much more than the differences.

Activity 4 Coming to terms with differing performing styles

Listen now to all the Examples. There is quite a range of performing styles represented, both in the pieces where the pupils are performing other people's music, and in those where they are performing their own or taking part in a performance of fellow-pupils' compositions. (Only Examples 7a and 7b are performed by teachers.) Which styles are you most at ease with, and which ones do you feel unfamiliar with or unable to assess? Are there performing qualities that you would listen for in any piece of playing or singing, whatever the style?

Specifically, compare the singing styles heard on the tape. Compare for example, the singer who sings the final example, 'The Schoolboy' (10b), the two girls singing 'Stewball' (2d), the pupil who sings 'Swing low' (5b(iii)), and the pupils improvising vocally on the 12-bar blues (3b). Are there any aspects of these vocal performances which to you are completely unacceptable (with regard to pitch, for example), or are you prepared to accept that there are different kinds of criteria with which to judge different styles? What does the term 'out of tune' mean to you? Are there instances on these recordings where a distinction can be made between singing that really is out of tune, and singing which intentionally 'bends' conventionally accepted pitches for an artistic purpose?

Will the performing options be open to pupils whose only experience of making music has been in the classroom?

The Criteria are emphatic that there should be continuity between classroom music-making and Music for GCSE:

> 1.2 A syllabus in Music for the GCSE must provide for courses which are a logical and practicable extension of work already done in the classroom.

And the assessment objectives in the Music Criteria stipulate that:

> 3. In the performing sections there will be those who receive instrumental tuition outside the GCSE course as well as those who have worked exclusively within the GCSE course; it must be possible for candidates who have received no instrumental tuition outside the GCSE course to achieve high grades in the examination.

Although classroom music-making is on the increase, the revolution has been a slow one. One of the factors said to have inhibited a wholeheartedly practical approach with the 11–14 age-group has been the academic emphasis of O-level, and the need many teachers have felt to prepare a minority for its rigours. With the Criteria positively welcoming a continuity of practical work throughout the 11–16 age-range, it is now possible to implement a policy of lively, varied and satisfying music-making throughout the secondary course as a whole.

Of all the activities covered in the performing component, only individual performance is not really appropriate to classroom work in the lower school. It may be possible to delegate much of the individual performing work to private or peripatetic instrumental teachers, but there will remain the task of organising suitable performing work for those who have not previously enjoyed the benefits of outside tuition. One solution might be to offer the opportunity to start an instrument 'from scratch' at the beginning of the 4th year. However, the teacher will still be left with the task of organising individual performing work for those pupils who find that none of the instruments offered by the school peripatetic system appeals to them. This will be less of a problem if a substantial amount of performing work has taken place in the earlier years, giving those who opt for GCSE a solid basis for performing during the course, without the benefit of individual tuition.

Many pupils of the GCSE age-group will have gained substantial performing skills outside the classroom without the benefit of organised instrumental tuition, especially those who have learnt to perform rock or folk music. Among this number, there will be pupils with the ability to achieve high marks for performing. They will need to be given challenges felt to be relevant, but that do not necessarily duplicate ones met outside the classroom.

Individual performing apart, all other sections of the performing component: ensemble work, group direction, sight-reading and echo-work, can be covered, or at least initiated, in the lower school classroom. Some of the simplest and most effective activities that can be done with a whole class can relate to the tasks set for unprepared performance, especially echo-work and improvisation.

Echo-work, the repetition of phrases clapped, sung or played by the teacher, is one of the basic classroom activities. It is essential to the patterning of songs taught by rote, and has a variety of other applications. Echo clapping alone can involve variables such as dynamics, tone colour (alternating clapping with snapping fingers and other body percussion sounds), texture (the addition of an ostinato accompaniment, which creates more interest while helping to maintain a steady pulse), and varied metrical patterns. It can be started as early as the infant school, and may be recapitulated at a variety of levels, including the start of the GCSE course. The advent of electronic keyboards with a facility for programming ostinati makes a further useful addition to the armoury of classroom instruments that can be brought into use at this stage.

Unpitched echo-work can be extended to embrace pitched work by using the singing voice and melodic percussion and recorders. It can also lead to improvisation. For instance, instead of echoing a phrase from the teacher, all pupils simultaneously could improvise an answer of equal length. The polyphony created by this means is interesting to listen to, and the exercise is good for giving pupils confidence to improvise, for no-one is singled out as a soloist at this stage. After becoming used to providing answer phrases in this way, responses from individuals can be sought. (A fuller account of ways of developing simple improvisation in class appears in the writer's article, 'The Blues, a practical project for the classroom' (1980, pp. 74–96). Imitative work in class can lead to improvising, and improvising, being the ready generation of ideas, can lead to composing.

Sight-reading can also be tackled as a classroom activity. Vocal methods such as those of Curwen and Kodály encourage both sight-singing and the cultivation of the inner ear through a judicious combination of sol-fa with staff notation. However, a course that was seen as entirely vocal might deter pupils, and so a balance of vocal and instrumental work is more desirable, for which, naturally, resources are required, on a par with any other subject pursuing practical work using apparatus.

Practical music-making in the full-sized class takes two forms: the 'rehearsal', in which a whole class sings a song or plays a piece under the teacher's direction; and the 'workshop', where a class is split into small working groups of up to six pupils. Workshop lessons do not *always* have to involve pupils composing or improvising; they are just as useful for tackling purely performing activities such as playing by ear, or working on small ensemble pieces using a mixture of unpitched and pitched instruments. The mode of working in small groups is closer to the requirements for ensemble performing at GCSE level than is the teacher-directed whole class 'rehearsal' mode, for individual parts can be readily identified and appraised. Example 2a, in which a group of pupils plays a version of the Largo from Dvorak's *New World* symphony, is an example of performing resulting from a 'workshop' lesson.

Rehearsing and directing can also be practised by pupils in lower school lessons. Not only can individuals be occasionally invited to lead whole-class performances, but it is a useful class-management tactic to appoint group leaders when working in the workshop mode, either on a performing or a composing project.

If instrumental work in the lower school is new to both teachers and pupils, it will need to be approached gradually. The addition of simple percussive ostinati to class songs is a manageable first step in this direction. (Hear Example 5a.) The gradual introduction of pitched instruments, initially to provide simple, repetitive accompaniment figures can, given time, develop into fully-fledged ensemble performing that is both attractive to listen to and rewarding to be involved in.

What is involved in unprepared performing?

Unprepared performance tests the candidate's ability to think on his or her feet musically. To an extent, it covers some of the same ground as aural dictation tests for O-level. The O-level aural examination tested two skills together – the accurate recall of musical phrases, and the ability to notate them. In the GCSE, care is taken to separate the two skills, so that an aurally acute pupil who does not read music is able to show his or her ability. The first option, sight-reading, is not compulsory, although the WJEC sets an additional sight-singing test which has to be taken by all candidates. The second option, echo-work, is compulsory only in the MEG(A) syllabus, and is, in any case, the option most likely to be chosen out of the three. Similar tests are set in the aural sections of the graded practical examinations, and the ablest candidates will be expected to provide instant and accurate recall of phrasing, dynamics and articulation, as well as the traditionally tested ones such as pitch and rhythm. The Grade descriptions given at the end of the Criteria show how differentiation may occur in unprepared performance:

Examples of Grade F attainment

A typical Grade F candidate is likely to have shown the ability to . . .
make a reasonable attempt to play short melodic phrases, e.g. a violinist would be required to use basic finger patterns in first position.

Examples of Grade C attainment

A typical Grade C candidate is likely to have shown the ability to . . .
play musical phrases noting performance detail, e.g. a violinist would be required to observe bowing, staccato and dynamic markings.

Both sight-reading and echo-work can be of value if they are part of the natural process of making music, and not treated simply as exercises in preparing for an examination. Good sight-reading is an admission ticket to all kinds of advanced ensemble performing, apart from being an enjoyable and stimulating intellectual challenge for its own sake. A good sight-reader, like an accurate echo-performer, will be able to encompass not only the notes played in correct time, but also the phrasing and the expression. A good sight-reader will be able to anticipate typical turns of phrase or harmonic progression, if the music is in a familiar style.

The third option, improvisation, should no more be compulsory than sight-reading, although the ability to improvise resembles the ability to sight-read in one important respect – that of thinking ahead. Improvisation has been encouraged much less than it might have been in traditional 'classical' music education, but a great many people who have learnt to perform in other styles and traditions are fluent and competent improvisers, with skills that are clearly worthy of recognition.

The principal benefit of unprepared performing should be to give the pupil the confidence to tackle musical tasks where quick, accurate thinking is required. The pupil should feel that sight-reading is a positive task, with the dots on the page representing real musical sounds, and not a struggle with some arcane irrelevance. Echo-work should not only extend the ability to memorise, and therefore make music more 'part of oneself', but it is also a necessary step to be taken before starting to improvise. The ability to improvise is likewise the first step towards learning to think like a composer. Composition is, after all, as has been said often, only slowed-down improvisation – less impulsive and more considered.

The following table gives the percentage mark weightings for prepared and unprepared performing for the different Group syllabuses.

Group	*Prepared*	*Unprepared*
LEAG	24	8
MEG (A)	22½	7½
MEG (B)	28.7 or 32.8	6.3 or 7.2*
NEA	24	6
SEG	24	6
WJEC	24	6
NISEC	27	8

*According to the weighting chosen, see Chapter 1, p. 11.

The mark for each option in unprepared performing ranges from 2% with the WJEC (remember: there are three tests – one compulsory sight-singing, and two options), to 4% with NISEC and LEAG. With the exception of the Midland Group, all syllabuses publish a table that gives an easily understood breakdown of the marking scheme. The MEG (B) syllabus, while commendably allowing weighting flexibility, has come up with what seems to be an unnecessarily fiddling scheme which is not easy to understand from reading the syllabus.

Although the Criteria allow for either internal or external assessment of performing, they give no indication as to who should set the unprepared performance tasks. All the Examining Groups have made the understandable assumption that the unprepared performing assessment should be in the form of tests set by the Board concerned, rather than being teacher-initiated tasks. This sets unprepared performing apart from the rest of the performing and composing components in all the Group syllabuses, so there follows a brief survey of the kind of tests likely to be set, based on a study of the specimen papers available at the time of writing.

LEAG

The tests cover a wide range of intruments, including pitched percussion, and the piano and organ tests are on two and three staves respectively. The echo-tests include examples for glockenspiel and steel pans. The melodic ideas for improvisation are somewhat less than inspiring, and there is no opportunity given to improvise over a chord sequence. However, the examiner may suggest an extra-musical stimulus for improvising, inviting the realisation in sound of a given title such as 'a procession' or 'evening'.

SEG

This follows a similar pattern to the other Groups. SEG gives a helpfully wide range of sight-reading examples, and the echo-tests are all taken from the repertoire. There is a wide choice for improvisation, ranging from making up a melody over a given accompaniment to improvising a short piece with a given title, such as 'The old man at rest'.

MEG (A)

The specimen echo-tests are very like similar kinds of tests for graded examinations. Despite the clear implication in the Criteria's Grade Descriptions that they should feature in the assessment, no indications of dynamics or articulation are present. The sight-reading tests consist of three items in a stepped scheme, with the more difficult items giving scope for dynamics and articulation. The ideas for improvisation consist of a rhythmic pattern, a limited group of notes and a chord sequence.

MEG (B)

The specimen sight-reading tests cover a range of instruments, and allow scope for 'folk' guitarists to accompany a given melody by making a suitable strum to the chords given. No specimen tests for echo-work are available. The ideas for improvisation include snatches of melody, a rhythmic figure, a chord sequence and a stimulus given in graphic notation.

NEA, WJEC and NISEC

These are similar to the other Groups. NEA offers a four-line stanza of verse as an optional improvisation stimulus. WJEC includes a compulsory sight-singing test, which may be whistled, or sung in tonic sol-fa.

Activity 5 Planning for the unprepared performing assessment

With your list of pupils again handy, tick off the two options each one is most likely to tackle out of the three available – sight-reading, echo-work, improvisation. Will you be able to organise help for any of these? For example, will any instrumental staff, either working for you in your school or known to you outside as coaching some of your GCSE students, be able to help with this?

---

3 Composing

What is composing for GCSE?

Composing is an activity where a person originates musical material, organising it into a form of his or her own choosing. Activities akin to composing have long featured in other 'Creative Arts' subjects, such as Drama, Visual Arts or 'creative writing' work in English and Welsh. However, they have never featured strongly in examination schemes for Music. From now on, composing will be a compulsory component in the GCSE.

The upgrading of composing is the most sweeping innovation in the Criteria. The idea that all children, given appropriately structured tasks, are capable of making up their own music, is not new. In the earlier years of the present century, Orff, Kodály and Yorke Trotter encouraged musical invention by children, with little response from the British examination system. The sea-change in attitude evident in the GCSE is the culmination of over thirty years of patient pioneering in classroom music, starting with teachers like John Paynter and Peter Maxwell Davies in the late 1950s who developed composing work with children across the ability range. During the 1960s, the classroom work of George Self and Brian Dennis, among others, incorporated idioms and techniques developed by those post-war 'classical' composers who were, at the time, perceived to be pushing back the frontiers of musical language. Further impetus to the 'creative' approach was given by the Schools Council Project: Music in the Secondary School Curriculum (1973–82), which gathered persuasive evidence that not only is composing a feasible classroom activity, but that it may possibly be the *most* valuable experience that we can offer to children in their general musical education. One teacher involved in the Project, Tom Gamble, has spoken and written eloquently in support of the 'creative' approach to class music:

> Musical activities in the classroom should include all three basic modes of musical experience – the creative, the recreative and the perceptual.
>
> But in my view creative activities in music are more educationally valuable, and for this reason they form a major part of the music syllabus at this school.
>
> Gamble, 1978, frames 3–4

On the other hand, many other teachers are nervous of the new emphasis, because they lack experience both of children and of themselves as composers. Examination syllabuses have not helped either, in the scant attention they have paid to the development of music during the present century and to the way composing, once regarded as a highly skilled and specialist activity, has become accessible to more people. Two things have contributed to bringing composing more within reach: one has resulted from developments in the way music can be stored and transmitted, and the other has resulted from developments in the language of music itself.

Until the invention of sound recording, the only way to store music was to notate it. 'Composing music', therefore, meant the same as 'writing music', a task demanding considerable expertise in handling notation. This is no longer necessarily the case. Nowadays, for example, jazz, rock and folk musicians rely more on recordings and the aural tradition for the transmission of their idioms than on notation. Most of the present-day rock-based styles of popular music grew out of the performing traditions established by jazz, where there is no clear separation between composer and performer. Jazz musicians, by virtue of their ability to improvise, are 'composers on their feet' as it were. Since the Beatles, it has been quite usual for rock musicians to perform their own material, and it is not surprising, therefore, that the idioms of present-day music provide such a rich fund of stylistic models for pupil composition.

Recent years have also seen the development of alternatives such as graphic notation which aims to convey timbre and textural density rather than the traditional parameters of melody, harmony and rhythm. Graphic notation has proved to be more immediate and accessible than staff notation as a means of conveying sound-patterns in certain idioms, and has been found very useful in the service of notating pupil compositions exploring tone-clusters and textures with an element of random organisation.

The emphasis on timbre and texture is but one facet of the way notation and other forms of musical storage have developed in the present century. But music itself has undergone a radical re-shaping. Until the beginning of this century, the only style recognised by the establishment was the European classical idiom characterised by tonality, smooth voice-leading, functional harmonic progression, modulation and the major–minor duality. It was thought necessary for students to train in the rigorous techniques of harmony and counterpoint in order to compose fluently and creatively. These forbidding requirements tended to isolate composers from other musicians, and made the study of 'composition' seem an arcane and highly specialised pursuit.

However, at the end of the nineteenth century, composers such as Debussy became aware of other musical traditions and absorbed many of their influences, weakening the monopoly of the European tradition. Drone and ostinato-based textures, making use of modes and other exotic scales outside the dual major–minor system, gave the music of Debussy, Ravel, Satie, Stravinsky and Bartók a new vitality and freshness. It was Carl Orff who first realised that many of these techniques could be used with children as a means of getting them to improvise melodic and rhythmic ideas, just as music educationists of a later generation were to base their classroom work on the idioms of the postwar European *avant garde*.

More recently, another factor has emerged to make composing even more accessible: microtechnology. The computer's ability to speed up processes that were once so laborious as to be out of reach of most people, and the synthesiser's instant access to a vast array of exciting timbres, is perhaps the most dramatic development of all in its implications for the future of music education. Creative musical activities, where young people are inventing and shaping their own pieces, are likely to proliferate in the years to come. Not to give composing the prominence it now has in music education would make the GCSE even more out of touch with musical reality in the final years of the twentieth century than was O-level until its demise.

What activities count as 'composing'?

The Criteria state that 'Candidates should be required to compose or arrange music in a traditional or in a contemporary idiom'. Note that they state 'compose *or arrange*.' Arranging is certainly a viable option for the composing component (Examples 5a–c). Later, the Criteria continue:

4.3 Composing includes pastiche and experimental work, free composition, melody writing, harmony, part-writing and arranging. Syllabuses must offer opportunities for all these and must be sufficiently flexible to take account of the broad spectrum of vocal and instrumental styles which candidates may wish to offer.

The following list contains suggestions for activities that may be classified as 'composing.' Some are very basic, others more complex and sophisticated, suitable only for the more able pupils. The traditional 'composing' exercises featured in O-level papers come somewhere in the middle of the range of difficulty.

Activities requiring only a limited range of skills, involving the generation and use of a single idea

- Making up a rhythmic pattern (unpitched).
- Making up an unpitched rhythmic ostinato pattern.
- Making up a group of unpitched ostinati that can be heard simultaneously to form a 'layered' texture.
- Adding a rhythmic ostinato accompaniment to a song.
- Making up a melodic ostinato pattern (using only a limited range of notes).
- Exploring the sonorities possible using a single sound-source.

Activities requiring the generation and use of a few ideas, suitable for group work

- Combining melodic with rhythmic ostinato patterns.
- Building a texture of layered melodic ostinati.
- Adding a melodic ostinato accompaniment to a song.
- Making up a melody using only a restricted range of notes (triad, pentatone), e.g. a fanfare.
- Any combination of one or more of the above activities, e.g. making up a simple melody and adding a rhythmic ostinato accompaniment.

Some of the above can be heard on the tape (Examples 4a–c and 5a–c).

Activities requiring a wider range of skills, which might grow out of the above beginnings

- Melodic composition:
  (i) Adding an answering phrase to a given opening.
  (ii) Single-line melody for one instrument or voice, showing awareness of basic melodic shapes and structure. The melody could be pentatonic, modal or tonal in the conventional sense (i.e. in either a major or minor key).
- Unaccompanied song, for solo voice, setting a text.
- A short piece showing awareness of timbre and texture (Example 4c).
- An arrangement of a folk song, using classroom instruments deployed simply (Example 5b(i–iii)).
- A short piece showing awareness of basic form (ternary, rondo), and the principles of repetition and contrast involved (Examples 4a, 4c(ii), 7a and 7b).

Activities involving the use of notation that can be pursued in relation to those on the first two lists

- Notating a rhythmic pattern.
- Notating a texture of unpitched rhythms (layered) in the form of a score. This is quite possible, providing not too much syncopation is involved.
- Notating a piece whose idiomatic emphasis is on texture, timbre and dynamics in the form of a graphic score.
- Notating a melody using a restricted range of pitches.

Activities suited to pupils who do not read staff notation, but who have a good range of musical skills, acquired largely by ear, without the help of instrumental lessons

- Composing a song, showing a feeling for melodic shape, musical organisation, word-setting and apt choice of chords. Song accompanied by guitar, keyboard or other combination of instruments.
- Instrumental piece, or a piece for an electronic medium such as a synthesiser, showing control, imagination and the ability to organise material within the chosen medium.

NB such activities will, in the absence of a notated score, require some form of annotation (Example 6). Songs should have their words written (Example 10a), and the addition of chord symbols (quite straightforward if the composer is also a guitarist or pianist) will also be a helpful feature of the presentation.

Activities suited to pupils who are able to read music, and who possess a good range of skills, acquired largely through 'traditional' instrumental teaching

All such pieces would be fully notated (Examples 7–9 and 10b). A wide range is possible, although for presentation purposes they should not be too ambitious either in scope or length. Songs, instrumental pieces, pieces for groups of instruments or voices, etc. Such pieces should show imaginative ideas and a grasp of musical organisation, harmony, part writing, instrumentation, etc.

It would be preferable for these compositions not to stay inanimate in just their notated form, but to be allowed to come to life in performance, and to be recorded for moderation purposes.

Pupils working at this level could also work melody-writing and harmony exercises (continuing a melody from a given opening, setting a text, harmonisation and part writing). Such exercises would be worthwhile, provided that the pupil's imagination was genuinely engaged and that there was an opportunity for the pupil to hear what had been written. Pupils with the ability to do well at 'harmony exercises' should nevertheless be encouraged to do more extended composing work, showing a grasp of longer forms such as strophic song, ternary, rondo or even variations. 'Arranging' is an example of a composing task that can be tried at a variety of levels, from the most basic (Example 5a), to the most elaborate (a fully-scored and elaborated arrangement for, say, a wind band). Example 5c falls in the middle of these two extremes, being an arrangement of a Christmas carol, worked out 'by ear' rather than notated. It should be remembered that arranging is a favourite activity of musicians, working in many different styles: classical, jazz and rock. There would be plenty of listening material available to support such a project, ranging from the 'Greetings Prelude', Stravinsky's astonishing and ingenious arrangement of 'Happy Birthday', to the pop LP 'Lennon and McCartney with a little Help from their Friends' (K Tel Records, NE 1317) which consists of Beatles songs in versions often radically different from the originals.

Activity 6 Planning your composing programme

What previous experience of composing or any other creative activity in Music, however simple, have members of your GCSE class done prior to joining the course? (An example might be improvising a short rhythmic pattern to accompany a song.) Have they done any creative music-making either (a) in the classroom, or (b) outside the classroom, e.g. work with electronic instruments at home, composing their own songs for pleasure, improvising in a pop group?

With your list of GCSE pupils available, write down any composing or other creative musical inclinations or experiences that you know the pupils may have already. What does this give you as a basis for further work?

Examples 3 and 5 are illustrations of tasks 'differentiated by outcome'; that is, a wide range of measured abilities are heard tackling the same creative challenge. Can you think of any other initial composing or improvising tasks for pupils in your group which will enable them to generate ideas and get simple pieces going?

In what way does GCSE differ from O-level work in melody writing, harmony and counterpoint?

Although one or two Boards allowed the optional submission of original compositions for consideration, the only O-level activities akin to composing were the melody-writing, part-writing and harmonisation questions set in the final timed papers. The area known as 'harmony and counterpoint' has always been contentious. It is worth recalling that in the 1960s, there was a previous upheaval in this area of musical study. To quote Paul Steinitz:

> 'Paper Work' Examinations are nearly everywhere gradually changing in character. Whereas a decade or two ago the great majority of university tests were specially composed in a style which, with its many restricting rules, was only found in textbooks, students are now more often examined on their knowledge of actual music.
>
> Steinitz, 1963, Introduction.

Steinitz's harmony and counterpoint textbooks were indicative of a new era of 'pastiche' or 'stylistic studies' where the student was set the task of reconstructing an extract of music from the past, either by harmonising a given treble (as in a Bach Chorale), or continuing from a given opening (of, for instance, a quartet minuet in the style of Haydn). This new approach to teaching harmony started in the universities and conservatoires in Britain, and eventually influenced GCE syllabuses, although some O-level boards continued to set tasks of the kind deplored by Steinitz right up to the very end. The revolution this time comes from the schools.

Although 'pastiche' harmony and counterpoint was an undoubted improvement, the scope and nature of the eventual assessment remained unchanged. Pastiche was 'a means of learning something about style', an activity purely for the benefit of the student working the exercise, and not a piece of original composing made up with an audience in mind. Final assessments nearly always took the form of timed written papers. Written in silence, and marked in silence by examiners unknown to the candidates, it is difficult to see how students or pupils could have perceived such tasks as having anything to do with musical communication.

Making composing a coursework undertaking enables pupils to test ideas aurally, and to modify them in the light of what they actually hear, rather than struggle to apply a dimly-understood set of 'rules' bearing little relation to their own musical experience. Only exceptionally gifted pupils will be able, like Mozart and Britten, to imagine and transcribe accurately entire pieces without the help of a sound-source. For most, the following description of trying out one's ideas must surely be more applicable:

> I know too, that the wish to imitate this music [*the street bands of St Petersburg*] led to my first efforts at composition; for I tried to pick out at the piano the intervals I had heard – as soon as I could reach the piano – but found other intervals in the process that I liked better, which already made me a composer.
>
> (Stravinsky, 1962, p. 21)

It is interesting to reflect that the adult Stravinsky's composing methods differed little in essence from the above description of his childhood experimentation at the piano. This serendipitous process is surely a more realistic model for composing than the writing of sterile exercises in an examination hall. The moment a pupil recognises a pattern chanced upon as pleasing, then a musical idea has germinated. Stravinsky's reminiscence also reminds us how composition develops naturally from imitation, a point to bear in mind when setting and assessing tasks in the early stages: we should not demand or expect originality until quite an amount of composing experience has been gained. Only then will a distinctive voice begin to show through.

It follows, then, that pastiche composition is perfectly acceptable for GCSE coursework, provided the candidate is happy thinking and working within the chosen style (Example 10a). But composing as *coursework*, whether it is original or consciously imitative of a style, should make the pupil more aware of its *purpose*. With the expectation that people known to him (his teacher, his GCSE classmates, his parents) will be the intended audience, the pupil is more likely to perceive composing as a piece of musical *communication*, rather than just an exercise. There is no reason why the skills intended to be acquired by working conventional harmony exercises cannot also be inculcated through coursework composing.

The coursework mode above all should enable pupils to get their compositions *heard*. Every effort should be made to get pupils' work performed. Two of the Examples, 7a and 7b, are even played by members of the school's peripatetic instrumental staff!

Activity 7

Do you have any pupils in your GCSE class likely to continue to A-level? What type of composing tasks do you plan to set them to ensure that the composing coursework component manages to stretch them? Listen to and study the scores of Examples 7–10. Has this composing work (mostly for GCSE) stretched the pupils concerned? Has it given them the opportunity to show themselves capable of musical achievements that the O-level 'paperwork' did not recognise or measure?

In what ways does composing for the GCSE differ from 'creative music' work done in the lower-school classroom?

The impetus for encouraging children to 'think like composers' came from pioneer educationists such as John Paynter writing in the late 1960s. The main innovation in class music was the *creative workshop*, where thirty pupils are divided into groups and assigned tasks designed to encourage the imaginative handling of sound materials. When organised with forethought by an inspiring teacher, both the workshop experience and the end-results could be very worthwhile.

The approach informed much of the philosophy of the Schools Council Project: Music in the Secondary School Curriculum (1973–82), and was a major factor influencing the drafting of the GCSE Criteria, with their emphasis on composing as an activity for all pupils. But there is a major difference between group composing and composing coursework for GCSE. Although neither the Music Criteria (nor, for that matter, the General Criteria) are explicit about the permissibility of collaborative work, all syllabuses stipulate that composing, like performing, must eventually focus upon individual attainment. Whether or not one supports this change of focus from collective to individual work on educational grounds, the fact remains that examinations as they are at present constituted need to assess and report on the achievements of individuals.

Group composing has proved to be so valuable in getting children used to generating ideas, organising them and communicating them to a known audience, that it should not be jettisoned completely at the start of a GCSE course, especially if this is the mode of working pupils have been used to in the lower school. Examples 4 and 5 contain group compositions worked either in the lower school or in the first year of a CSE Mode III course, and joint authorship is claimed for Examples 6 and 8, both compositions forming part of course-work folios. However, this mode of working has to be replaced gradually by individual composing during the GCSE course, so that a final assessment and grading of a pupil's identifiable work can be made.

As in all other subjects studied for GCSE, work cannot be completed in the classroom alone. Pupils must get used to the idea of composing for homework or in preparation time, and will need some kind of sound-source on which to test their ideas.

Activity 8 ***Observing the emergence of pupils' ideas for composing***

Listen to Examples 5a–c. They are what jazz and pop musicians call 'head arrangements', that is, arrangements composed by ear, often collaboratively during rehearsal, but not committed to manuscript. Examples 5a and b are results of classroom group work; 5c is an individual effort.

To count as a composition, an arrangement must have some creative input from its arranger(s). As you listen to the tape, write down a brief description of the one main idea that each arrangement contributes to make its version of the given material distinctive.

How much composing work has to be submitted?

With composing a major new factor in GCSE, there has been an understandable tendency for teachers to take fright at the seemingly overwhelming requirements of an apparently limitless canvas of composing genres with their attendant range of differing assessment techniques. It is worth keeping a cool head and examining syllabuses to find out exactly how much assessed composing work will actually need to be submitted for moderation:

LEAG:	two to four pieces, with a combined duration not exceeding ten minutes.
SEG:	the candidate will select work representing a minimum of five minutes playing time.
MEG (A):	at least two pieces, lasting five to ten minutes in total.
MEG (B)	no specification as to quantity or timing. 'The candidate selects work to be assessed from work done during the course.'
NEA:	playing time need not normally exceed five minutes.
WJEC:	a selection of coursework, which need not exceed five minutes.
NISEC:	the total playing time of the final submission should be approximately five minutes.

In general, this means two to four pieces, selected from a larger number completed by the pupil over the two years of the course. Viewed in this light, the composing requirements are perhaps not as awe-inspiring as they might at first seem.

Do all compositions have to be notated by the pupil for presentation?

The National Criteria make the following stipulation about the presentation of compositions:

> 4.3.1 Candidates should be allowed to use the form of notation appropriate to the music they are composing: submissions need not be restricted to folios of notated music if annotated tapes are found to be more suitable.
>
> 4.3.2 A score and/or a recording of the candidate's composition(s) or arrangement(s) must be available.

The Criteria are at pains to broaden the definition of composing to make it mean more than simply *writing* music. For a number of contemporary styles, including those derived from a predominantly aural tradition, tape may be a more representative means of preserving the music in permanent form. However, there is an implication in the Criteria, which many Examining Groups have taken up, that *where appropriate*, scores should be submitted, and that additional credit will be gained by the candidate for competence in handling notation accurately. Examples 7, 8, 9 and 10b clearly derive not only from their composers' experience as listeners, but also from their years of learning to play their instruments while at the same time learning to read staff notation. For them, the handling of notation is indeed a positive achievement.

Where scores are neither possible nor indeed appropriate, the Criteria suggest that 'annotated tapes' may be substituted. Most syllabuses make annotation a requirement if a score is not submitted (Example 6).

The Criteria do not specify whether annotations should be prepared by the pupil or the teacher, but most syllabuses require annotations from pupils, giving a brief indication of the intention of the work, and appending the words if a text is set. No stipulation is given as to whether annotations will be assessed

Group	*Tape*	*Scores*	*Annotations by pupil*	*Annotations by teacher*
LEAG	Compulsory for all composing work (?) Some contradiction between pp. 3 and 15	To be presented as appropriate. Some doubt (p. 15) as to whether recording is compulsory	If score not presented	Not required
SEG	Recording encouraged but not compulsory	Not compulsory if style inappropriate	Compulsory, *whether or not* score is submitted	Teacher required to take note of process
MEG (A)	Compulsory only if score not submitted	Not compulsory if style inappropriate	Compulsory only if score not submitted	Not required
MEG (B)	Compulsory only if score not submitted	Not compulsory if style inappropriate	Compulsory only if score not submitted	Teacher required to record process as well as give final assessment
NEA	Compulsory only if score not submitted	Not compulsory if style inappropriate	Compulsory only if score not submitted 'Coursework cover sheet' (p. 31) to be completed	Teacher required to make notes on the 'candidate internal assessment form'
WJEC	Compulsory only if score not submitted	Not compulsory if style inappropriate	Compulsory only if score not submitted. Annotations may be in written or spoken form (on tape)	Aspects of the process should be noted on the mark sheet
NISEC	Compulsory only if score not submitted	Not compulsory if style inappropriate	Compulsory only if score not submitted	Not required

for quality and appropriateness in the same way as scores. One Examining Group, the WJEC, allows annotations to take the form of spoken introductions on tape. The table on page 35 summarises the composing presentation requirements of the different Examining Groups.

What is the teacher's role in the supervision of coursework?

Just as a piece of coursework must be identifiable as the pupil's own, and not as an indivisible collaboration with another pupil, so the teacher must report all aspects of coursework in which help has been given. This task is known as 'Authentication':

> Steps must be taken to ensure either that the work submitted is that of the candidate concerned or, if it is acceptable for the candidate to be given help by the teacher or in other ways, that any such assistance is recorded and taken into account in making the assessment.
>
> from General Criteria, 40.

The General Criteria, furthermore, suggest two kinds of Authentication:

> (a) a declaration by the candidate that he or she has produced the work involved without external assistance (apart from any which is acceptable under the scheme of assessment and is recorded);
>
> (b) a declaration by the teacher that the candidate's activities were kept under regular supervision and that to the best of his or her knowledge, no assistance has been given apart from any which is acceptable under the scheme of assessment and has been identified and recorded.
>
> from General Criteria, 40.

Where composing coursework is concerned, the following assistance may be given to candidates, *provided it is recorded in the assessment*:

- *Giving a musical stimulus to start off a piece*, e.g. a short melodic phrase to continue.
- *Help and suggestions at a point where a pupil has got 'bogged down'*. This may consist of encouraging the pupil to see the composing work in an entirely new light, such as changing the vocal or instrumental medium for which, so far, it has been conceived.
- *Help with notating the piece*. This may range from correcting small 'spelling errors' such as accidentals (see the G sharps in the score of Example 7a) to much more substantial help with a pupil who has real difficulty in handling notation. In an extreme case, a teacher might wish to notate an entire piece for the pupil, but it would be probably more appropriate to present it as an annotated recording.
- *Help with written annotation*. The teacher may suggest the use of some generally accepted technical terms in a pupil's annotation to help clarify the pupil's working method and growth of insight.
- *Help with presentation*. The teacher will naturally wish to secure a recording of as good a quality as possible. Cassette recorders with inbuilt microphones are not recommended for this purpose, as too much motor noise tends to get picked up. A good quality cassette or reel-to-reel recording, preferably in stereo, should be obtainable using equipment available in most schools these days. Some LEAs have their own studios, where a range of more sophisticated equipment may be available. Where the teacher makes musical recommendations about balance and location in a studio recording, these should be entered on the assessment as part of the help given.

One or two suggestions may be appropriate here about the physical presentation of the folio. One neat and convenient form of coursework folder would be in the form of an A4 ring-binder, with the compositions or annotations written on either MS or ordinary lined paper, and a cassette of all the pupil's compositions fixed inside the cover. A number of stationers supply A4-sized 12-stave hole-punched MS paper, which should be adequate for most composing coursework purposes unless scoring for a large ensemble is called for. The compositions should be in correct order on the tape, to correspond with the order of presentation in the folder, and the insert card of the cassette should also be clearly labelled, with the individual pieces itemised. Not only should scores be legible and unambiguous, but the tapes should be carefully edited for presentation. Spoken inserts announcing the pieces are very helpful, and indeed are essential if the annotations are to be spoken ones, as permitted by the WJEC.

What kind of composing task can be set for GCSE?

Composing is the most individualised of all activities for GCSE, and pupils will differ considerably in their attitudes and approaches to this part of the examination. Some will be highly motivated to compose, and may be prepared to select their own challenges. For example, a pupil who, before starting the GCSE course, has already demonstrated a flair for songwriting, should be encouraged to continue this self-chosen pursuit. This does not mean, however, that the teacher does not have a role in task-setting. The teacher's wider knowledge and experience may enable the pupil to see songwriting in an entirely new light - suggesting a new kind of text to set, or asking for the songs to fit into an extended pattern such as a song cycle or a 'musical' show.

A majority of pupils, however, will need more specific guidance, and there follows a suggested pattern for working a project over a period of 3 to 4 weeks during the first term of the GCSE course.

Rhythm, repetition and texture

This assignment can be worked through at all levels of ability. The end-product of the assignment will be a piece using the ostinato principle in some way.

The first lesson concentrates on listening, to provide models and a stimulus for pupils' own ideas. In preparation for this lesson, the teacher will have selected a number of varied extracts of music which demonstrate the use of the ostinato principle. The ones selected as an initial stimulus should be simple in character, conveying a clear idea of the nature of the practical assignment that will follow. More complex and sophisticated examples can be used as a follow-up to the finished project, when all pupil assignments have been completed, performed and recorded. Many pop records exemplify the simple building up of texture through the use of short repeated motifs, but examples can be found in a wide variety of styles. The opening of 'The snow is dancing' from Debussy's *Children's Corner* suite for piano is a delightful example of the proliferation of a 'layered texture' through the superimposition of a number of ostinato patterns. Its expressive effect is to conjure up a visual image: initially a sparse flurry of just a few flakes, with the air becoming denser with snow as the fall progresses. Ostinato-based textures are a feature of the 'impressionist' style, and one might invite a comparison with the use of superimposed 'riffs' in pop music, which resemble the music of Debussy, Satie and Ravel in that they tend to be modal rather than diatonically tonal. 'The snow is dancing' opens in the Aeolian mode, and there is a translucent mixture of active ostinati and sustained notes holding the texture together.

To take a more recent example from the world of popular music, Isaac Hayes' theme music for the film 'Shaft' is a fascinating example of a texture held together by a strong rhythmic pulse, yet composed of a number of disparate elements. The texture mixes unpitched percussion sounds with the pitched sounds of electric guitar, bass guitar and orchestral instruments. Starting with an active quaver pattern on hi-hat and a fragmentary riff on guitar, the texture builds, carefully and artfully contrasting active elements with sustained chords and pedal notes. The music, like Debussy's, is intended to be evocative, and seems to convey an image of both the grandeur and the bustle, and also some of the menace of a big city. 'Shaft' also resembles the impressionist idiom in that it is modal and drone-based, oscillating slowly between two sustained chords – Fmaj7 and Em7, yet with a seeming tonal focus on G, giving the music a Mixolydian modal flavour.

The lesson would start, then, with a playing and discussion of pieces which start with a build-up of repetitive patterns. There would be some discussion of the expressive effect it has (e.g. evoking the snow, its coldness, its gentleness and gathering thickness in the Debussy; the spaciousness and bustle of the Isaac Hayes) and the means of achieving the effects (use of contrasting elements – sustained sounds contrasted with more lively patterns, pitched with unpitched, varied tone-colours). The clarity of both is obtained by mixing together very disparate sounds.

Next, the class could work together with the teacher to build up an ostinato texture. Either the whole class could be involved, if the group is not a large one, or a small group (say, three pupils) could work with the teacher as a 'demonstration group.' The teacher would start things going by improvising a short pattern – pitched or unpitched – and other members of the group would add to this, one by one, until a texture was 'up and running'. This activity provides a transition stage between the initial stimulus provided by the listening, and the practical work that is to follow.

The next stage would consist of a group composing project, worked in lesson time. The class, divided into groups of 3 to 5 pupils, is set to compose collective ostinato pieces. A variety of resources can be used: body percussion sounds (hands, fingers, clicking tongues, etc.), unpitched percussion and pitched instruments of all kinds, including electronic if available. The latter might be especially suitable, if they can be programmed to produce ostinati. But beware – the teacher needs to be sure that it is the pupils not the machines that are doing the musical thinking!

At the end of the working session, the pieces are stored by means of tape recording. At the beginning of the next lesson, the recordings are played back, discussed constructively and, where possible, notated in the form of a score.

Pupils are now set individual assignments to compose ostinato pieces – pieces making use of rhythmic or melodic repetition in some way. These may be started in the remainder of time available for the lesson, but should be continued for homework. (The term 'homework' is used here in its broadest sense, and should be taken to imply also 'preparation time' in boarding schools. Pupils may wish to work at breaks or after school, using the sound-resources available on the school premises, rather than work at home, which pupils who are inner-city flat dwellers may find difficult.) Such pieces could be wholly electronic (in which case the use of recording overdubbing may come in useful), could be for a solo instrument such as a piano (like Example 9c)), or be for a group of performers, most easily the other members of the GCSE class, in which case the 'composing' activity must include the giving of clear instructions to the participants. This is most easily done in the form of a notated score, but there are other ways.

The individually composed pieces should be ready for the next lesson, where they should be performed and recorded. The final session, following this, should involve playback of these individual pieces, and also more listening to pieces demonstrating the use of ostinato, or indeed, broadening this out to repetition in music generally. Stan Getz's *bossa nova* piece 'Desafinado' or the lively second movement of Debussy's String Quartet are further examples that could be used. Material for 'asssociated listening', could be easily found among the 'set works' prescribed for the listening component by a number of Examining Groups. Here is a list of works prescribed for 1988 which contain movements exemplifying the use of repetition or ostinato:

LEAG: A group of songs by the rock band Genesis is set.
WJEC: The Beatles *Help!* LP. The song 'Ticket to ride' opens with an accumulation of riffs (ostinati) over a pedal point.
NISEC: Stravinsky's *Symphony of Psalms*. There are marvellous examples of layered textures and ostinati in the outer two movements. The middle movement demonstrates another principle of repetition – a fugue.

There follows a summary of this suggested project. It is assumed that each session incorporating both composing and performing will take a double period, and that each session involving composing only will take about 55 minutes of a 70 minute session.

Session One: Listening as a stimulus to get the project going. Simple, even primitive examples of the use of repetition in music. Class works with teacher to build layered texture. Groups now work to produce layered ostinato pieces. These are recorded on tape.

Session Two: Group compositions played back. Some attempt at notation (if appropriate). Individual assignments to compose ostinato pieces now set. These are worked on by pupils for homework/ preparation for the next lesson.

Session Three: Pupil ostinato compositions performed and recorded.

Session Four: Playback of individual compositions, followed by associated listening, taken from set works or other appropriate source.

Activity 9

Plan a composing 'module' for your GCSE group, using as a model the plan worked out for the 'Repetition' project. Choose listening material for modelling and follow-up reinforcement, and plan the range of activities carefully so that they last over a period of weeks. Ensure that your project is devised so that each pupil is eventually able to produce his or her own individual piece.

Topics you might consider include: composing a melody, composing a song, arranging an existing piece or song, exploring musical form (e.g. rondo, ternary, variations), exploring a particular medium (composing a 'study' for a particular instrument might be an example of this), or exploring an extra-musical stimulus (providing music to accompany a text, or a piece of film).

PART 2 Examples of pupils' work

The pages which follow detail the Examples of pupils' music-making work heard on the tape accompanying this booklet. Not all of them are by GCSE pupils working in years 4 and 5. A number were collected from pupils studying music on Mode III CSE courses pioneered during the 1970s. Others, while they exemplify tasks that might indeed be set as GCSE coursework, come from 'lower-school' classes (that is, years 1–3 secondary, pupils aged between 11 and 14 years).

Where appropriate, scores of these compositions appear in this part of the book, in a facsimile of the pupils' own handwriting. Where possible, I have appended annotations made, in most cases, by the teachers concerned.

Most of the recordings were made in classroom conditions, and are limited by the acoustics, instruments and equipment available.

1 Performing

1 Solo performance

These were all recorded at interim assessment sessions for fourth year secondary pupils doing the GCSE course for the first time (1986–88). They represent the work of pupils who have received 'classical' instrumental tuition, either privately or through the LEA-based peripatetic system.

(a) Study in D by Heller, for piano; interpretations by two different pupils.
(b) Hymn tune, 'All creatures of our God and King', played on the trombone.
(c) 'Trumpet tune' by Purcell; two performances, played by the same pupil on cornet.
(d) Slow movement of 'cello sonata by Willem de Fesch, with piano accompaniment.
(e) Chopin, Prelude in C minor for piano.

2 Group performance

None of these illustrations is from a current GCSE class, but they exemplify ensemble activities that could be pursued in a GCSE course. In contrast to the individual performances above, most of the pupils here did not acquire their vocal or instrumental skills through the 'conventional' system of LEA-organised teaching or private lessons.

(a) Theme tune from the Largo of Dvorák's *New World* symphony (lower-school class group)

This is an example of ensemble performing resulting from group work in a lower-school class which had previously been introduced to the piece through listening to a recording. The class had been split into smaller groups, and set the task of working out the notes of the melody in order to perform a simplified arrangement of the Dvorák using the instruments available. This particular group featured pitched percussion (including a prominent ostinato figure for bass xylophone), and a flute, played by a pupil who had only been learning the instrument for a few weeks. None of the other pupils involved had had any experience of instrumental playing away from the classroom. A great deal of playing by ear was involved in putting this performance together, for, apart from the beginner flautist, none of the pupils could have learnt this purely from the notation.

(b) 'Dido's Lament' by Purcell, performed by oboe, saxophone, piano and bass guitar

This is an example of an *ad hoc* ensemble, arising from the kind of assorted groupings of pupils one might well find in a GCSE class. The recording was made by a CSE group following a Mode III syllabus which had a strong performing component. Each individual instrument can be heard clearly, enabling individual assessments to be made, if needed. The recording shows pupils of disparate musical backgrounds and interests working together in a co-operative venture, initiated by their teacher who played the piano in the ensemble.

(c) Group performance (two performers), improvisation over a repeated chord progression; drummer, accompanied by keyboard player, reggae style

Two takes were recorded, the first using piano, the second an electronic organ. However, the principal participant is the drummer, while the keyboard simply lays down a brief chord progression, as follows:

B♭ / / / Cm / / / E♭ / F / B♭ / F /

The recording highlights an instrument previously given little recognition in examination circles, due to the traditional 'Western' prejudice about the status of unpitched instruments, and indeed unpitched sounds in music generally. This is the first of the recordings to feature improvisation, and, quite possibly stimulated by the change of accompanying instrument, the drummer comes out with new ideas in the second take.

(d) Irish-American folk song, 'Stewball', performed by two girls, singing in harmony, and accompanying themselves on guitars

Two pupils who, like the bass guitar player in the Purcell and the drummer in the duet improvisation, developed their performing skills without the help of organised instrumental teaching. The song was picked up from a recording, with the guitar chords learnt as a means of accompanying the singing. In the second verse, the voices split into two parts in a characteristic 'folk' manner.

3 Examples of improvisations over the same chord pattern, exemplifying differentiation by outcome

The last examples of performing work consist of a series of short recordings of improvisations upon that archetype of twentieth century popular musical forms, the 12-bar blues. A wide range of abilities is represented, and, apart from showing that the blues is a style in which children can improvise comfortably, the extracts exemplify *differentiation by outcome*, that is, the same task performed by pupils of widely differing abilities.

The recordings may help to clarify the term 'improvisation'. The blues is a well known pattern, so, in a sense, these are not 'unprepared' performances. Jazz and rock improvisers more often make something new out of an existing, often well known, song or chord-pattern, rather than create music entirely afresh.

The term 'chorus' means one cycle of the chord progression on which the improvisation is based. At least two choruses of the blues are presented on each of these Examples, either consecutively or from separate recorded 'takes', in order to show the process of improvisation taking place.

(a) A lower-school pupil playing a pentatonic bass xylophone in a class ensemble performance

Two takes of this solo are presented. This was part of a performance in which a number of pupils took turns to contribute 12-bar improvisations over the blues chord-sequence. Two pupils from the class, who played in a rock band outside school, provided a stylish backing on electric guitar and bass:

(b) A vocal blues: some 'scat' singing by three 15-year old girls

Here, the 12-bar pattern is split into three phrases, and each pupil takes a turn to improvise four bars. As before, two 12-bar sequences are presented, and they demonstrate not only the emergence of fresh ideas in the second take, but also marked differences of ability and approach between the three performers.

(c) A piano 'boogie woogie'

Performed by a pianist who was also Grade V standard in the 'classical' repertoire.

(d) Blues played on a solo acoustic guitar

Three choruses of the blues improvised by a self-taught guitarist, aged 16.

2 Composing

4 Group compositions by lower-school pupils

(a) A pentatonic melody in ABABA form for glockenspiel and metallophone, composed jointly by two lower-school pupils

A straightforward example of collaborative work by pupils in a lower-school class. The melody uses a restricted set of notes – the 'sharps' (that is, the pentatonic part) of a metallophone and a glockenspiel.

(b) A piece for recorders and pitched percussion

A group piece that combines improvising with composing. Four of the five pupils, playing bass xylophone, metallophone, glockenspiel and treble recorder, weave a 'layered' texture consisting mostly of broken chord ostinati. The mixture of G and C triads gives a mildly bitonal flavour to the harmony, which is static and non-functional. Over this, a descant recorder improvises quite freely.

(c) Two pieces exploring a variety of timbres and patterns possible using a single sound source: (i) a cymbal, (ii) an old piano frame

These are short pieces which build patterns out of timbres rather than pitches. Gamble (1982, p. 187), has suggested that such a project might be a useful starting point for creative work, linked to listening to music in contemporary idioms and oriental music.

5 Examples of 'head arrangements', that is, arrangements composed by ear rather than notated or transcribed

(a) Of 'Michael row the boat ashore', by a group of lower-school pupils

This is another example of an 'early' creative project that is possible using an absolute minimum of resources. The group sang and added unpitched accompaniments, using clapping and the tables in the classroom as the 'percussion'. Such a project can be worked upon for a very short period of time during a lesson.

(b) Of 'Swing low', three arrangements by groups of lower-school pupils

These are three straightforward group arrangements using instruments available in the classroom:
(i) for three xylophones;
(ii) for three xylophones and bongoes;
(iii) for voice, drums and bongoes.

(c) Of 'God rest you merry, gentlemen', by a fourth year pupil, for voice and piano

6 A piano duet, composed by two girls who perform it on this recording

This piece was not notated by the composers, but they both made written annotations. Here is the annotation made by the *seconda* player, who performed most of the piece:

March 4th 1986.

A Duet With a Difference!

Unlike piece number one, there are two people - Samantha and myself. This composition took longer to complete, as there is a different sound in contrast altogether.

The composition begins in a major key and after a repeat turns into a minor key.

To start the piece off, I played firstly, followed by an echo, played by Samantha. It was decided early on, that the piece should concentrate particularly on 'echos'. Throughout the entire composition this can be heard.

Although the piece sounds rather 'simple', it took a fair time to complete, roughly about four weeks.

Within the piece, we used chords, broken chords and simple single notes. The piece was eventually recorded on March 4th 1986.

The piece of music started with me playing C, E, G, A, G, E twice, and Samantha repeating this an octave HIGHER. Then, we played the same (major chord would be formed) notes together twice, but, when I played these notes a third time, Samantha played C, E♭, G, A♭, G, E♭, twice, forming an unusual sound - one major set of notes being played with a set of minor notes. This pattern can be heard about three times.

After a series of patterns, I played notes on the piano lower down, forming a sequence of Arpeggios at times. E.g.

I played a B major arpeggio: B, D♯, F♯, B and gradually this turned minor. To continue the sequence, I played just an A major arpeggio, and then I reverted back to the beginning, again going up in step. All of this is repeated up until the second lot of arpeggios, where we both end the piece.

The actual form of this piece is Ternery.

Annabel Walley.

7 Two pieces by the same pupil: (a) rondo for solo flute, and (b) a rondo for flute and bassoon

Both pieces are accompanied by scores in the pupil's own hand. The performances heard on the tape are by members of the instrumental teaching staff at the school concerned.

Rondo for Flute and Bosoon by Rhys Davies
Allegro
mf
Legato
mp.
mf
mp.

mf
mf
mf
mf cresc.
F
On the last note C may be played instead of G natural

8 A duet for flute and clarinet, jointly composed and performed by the composers

3
3
3
3
3
3
3
3

9 Three piano pieces, GCSE submissions, composed and played by fourth year pupils from the same class, with scores

(a) 'Sunrise'; (b) 'A prelude'; (c) 'Infinity'.

pp
pp
pp
pp
pp

p
p
8va
mf
3
mf.
rit.
ppp.
ppp.

A Prelude
by Sally Gull

Infinity by Kathryn Tinkler
LARGO.
pp
mp

10 Two songs, with piano accomaniment

(a) 'I was wrong', words and music by the same pupil for two voices with piano.
(b) 'The Schoolboy', setting of the poem by William Blake, for solo voice and piano.

Here are the words to the two songs:

I Was Wrong

I was wrong, you were right,
I know that now the time we lost was only a night,
The thought of knowing, that after all we said,
The times we laughed, the times we cried
Are all now dead.
And I love you.
Love me too
Love me true.

I needed time to sort things out.
I walked away and left you there,
I'll never forgive myself,
How could I go, when you had cried?
I never thought of my mistake
Until my anger died.
And I love you.
Love me too
Love me true.

I turned around, I headed back
To where I'd left you all alone,
But you had gone.
I heard the roar, and saw the lights,
The flashes of blue still in my mind,
They took you away from me.
And I love you.
Love me too
Love me true.

by Elizabeth Lane

The Schoolboy

I love to rise in a summer morn
When the birds sing on every tree;
The distant huntsman winds his horn,
And the skylark sings with me.
O! what sweet company.

But to go school in a summer morn,
O! it drives all joy away;
Under a cruel eye outworn
The little ones spend the day
In sighing and dismay.

Ah! then at times I drooping sit,
And spend many an anxious hour,
Nor in my book can I take delight,
Nor sit in learning's bower,
Worn thro' with the dreary shower.

How can the bird that is born for joy
Sit in a cage and sing?
How can a child when fears annoy
But droop his tender wing
And forget his youthful spring?

O! father and mother, if buds are nip'd
And blossoms blown away,
And if the tender plants are strip'd
Of their joy in the springing day,
By sorrow and care's dismay,

How shall the summer arise in joy,
Or the summer fruits appear?
Or how shall we gather what griefs destroy,
Or bless the mellowing year
When the blasts of winter appear?

William Blake, 1794

For technical reasons it has only been possible to include the first three verses of the Blake setting on the tape, although the entire song is printed here in facsimile:

Verse 2. But to go to school in a sum- mer morn O! it drives all joy a-
" 5. on Fath-er and moth-er if buds are nip'd And bloss-oms blown a-
way Und-er a cru - el eye out- worn The lit-tle ones
way And if the tend- er plants are strip'd Of their joy in the
spend the day In sigh - ing and dis- may.
spring-ing day By sorr-ow and care's dis- may.

V3: Ah! then at times droop-ing sit And spend man-y an anx - ious
hour Nor in my book can I take de - light Nor
sit in learn - ings bower Worn through with the drea ry
shower.

Verse 4:
How can the bird that is born for joy
Sit in a cage and sing?
How can a child when fears an-noy
But droop his tend - er wing
And for- get his youth- ful spring?

PART 3 Assessment

1 Assessment defined

Coursework assessment may involve the appraisal of any combination of practical performing or composing assignments at regular intervals throughout the course. It may range from a recorded rehearsal where pupils are working on a group performance to an individual's completed composition recorded onto tape and fully notated.

Musical assessment is a complex process. At present there is a requirement for all assessments to be presented ultimately in the form of a numerical mark. This is clearly unsatisfactory, and bears no relation to the 'real' world of music, where assessments (such as a review of a concert) tend to take the form of a verbal profile. There is a move afoot towards establishing verbal profiling in the form of 'records of achievement' covering all aspects of a pupil's school career:

> Records of achievement will supplement, and may well eventually replace, external examination certificates. A pupil's Record will attempt to give a full positive picture of that child. It will show his or her achievements over a whole range of activities taking place in and out of school . . .
>
> Teachers will see little point in making two assessments – one for the GCSE and one for the Record of Achievement – of essentially the same achievement. The GCSE and Records of Achievement need to be compatible, and the GCSE may well therefore need to adapt if it is not to be antipathetic to this new initiative.
>
> From Mobley *et al.*, 1986, p. 140

Maybe this is good news for music education, as there has always been an unease about giving marks for aesthetic achievement, where the variables to be assessed combine in such a subtle and complex manner and so much also depends on subjective judgements. Even those who organise traditional examining schemes such as the local grade examinations have been conscious that marks alone are unsatisfactory. Hence the examiners' assessment forms which are returned to parents and teachers containing written comments on the performance, as well as numerical marks. However, for the time being, numbers and grades are a fact of life in GCSE assessment in all subjects, and so this part of the book will address ways of dealing with these for both performing and composing.

I would suggest that there are four levels on which we can exercise our musical judgement, whether of composing or of performing. The first level, the one that O-level and CSE have traditionally addressed, is that of undisputable musical fact. In performing, for example, this would be to assess the extent to which a candidate plays the correct notes in the correct rhythm, as given by the notated text of the music. Many tests traditionally set for CSE and O-level were not directly related to the making of music but were instead concerned with eliciting answers that could be marked as either right or wrong. Aural dictations and questions eliciting factual information abut composers endured in examination papers, not because they were able to pick up any artistic response but because their assessment was a straightforward matter.

Music examinations, instead of being true to the often elusive nature of music, have tended to seek 'respectability' by trying to fit into the culture of 'The Three "R"s', a culture most at home with the measurable and unambiguous world of words and numbers, where the eyes rather than the ears are the principal recipients of information. Hence the importance attached to notation. Despite the reforms initiated by the Criteria, there remains a timidity on the part of some Examining Groups to accept wholeheartedly those forms of music-making that are not backed up by visual evidence or verbal explanation. To quote Erwin Stein: 'Quite at home as we are in the world of the eye, the realm of the ear is a fairly strange country. Before the eye, things are firm and lasting, but to the ear everything seems loose and fleeting.'

This brings us to the second level of assessment, which concerns those aspects of sound which, though palpable, are not readily or precisely described by notation or technical language. In fully notated idioms, if we are in possession of a score it is easy to assess whether a performer is playing all the correct notes in the right time. However, there are many other equally important aspects of sound which cannot be notated so precisely. 'Correct notes in the correct time' does not necessarily indicate that a performance has conveyed the relationships between the notes – whether the notes are being sung or played *in tune*, and at a tempo which allows the rhythm to breathe naturally. Dynamics, articulation, phrasing and tone colour are all aspects of music which tend to be notated ambiguously and are therefore open to interpretation. Ambiguity is part of the nature of art, and it is precisely at the moment when music gets interesting that examination assessment has tended to come to a stop, because assessment beyond this point is perceived as a 'matter of opinion.'

Similarly with composing, examinations have tended to concentrate more on aspects that can be assessed easily, such as the precision with which the candidate has notated an exercise, or the way known 'rules' of harmony or part-writing have been observed. Examinations have tended to disregard those idioms and aspects of music, such as timbre or texture, that are not so readily open to being notated.

The assessment of improvisation, which is a hybrid of performing and composing, may pose special problems for teachers used to music fixed in the form of notation. Although it is an option attracting only a few marks in the GCSE, improvisation can be of enormous help in enabling pupils to generate ideas for composing. For this reason, improvisation has a rather higher profile in this book than it does in the actual examination at present. Discussion of improvisation will feature in both the chapters on assessing performing and on assessing composing.

The third level of assessment concerns the personal preferences of the person doing the assessing. Teachers will need to keep a sense of proportion about these in order to admit musical accomplishment in styles that are unfamiliar, or even alien to them. It is universally acknowledged that the more one listens to the unfamiliar in music, the more one is able to discern the nature of its content and the intentions of the composer or improvising musician who created it. This is why coursework assessment is so important, especially for composing, because it enables the teacher to get to know the musical thinking and the musical preferences of the pupil concerned, and can lead to mutual understanding. The pupil must grow to understand that he or she has an audience to communicate with, and must be able to respect the teacher as a musically perceptive representative of that audience, and the teacher likewise needs to grow in understanding of the way the pupil thinks musically.

The fourth level of assessment concerns process. Besides becoming more aware of the wide range of variables involved in the appraisal of performance, teachers will also need to ask questions such as 'What is the pupil learning from this task, what musical skills are being developed, what worthwhile knowledge, what experiences?' Where composing is concerned, a single piece of work may seem incomplete or unprepossessing if judged simply as an end-product, but it may have a story to tell about how a pupil has developed through undertaking the task, and its relationship to other tasks. The educational principle which lays stress on the *process* as well as on the end-product applies not just to Music, but underpins the approach of the GCSE across the whole curriculum.

Activity 10

Listen to the recorded illustrations accompanying this booklet. Which ones would you feel most at home assessing, and with which would you find most difficulty in coming to terms?

---

2 Assessing performing

What does the assessment of performing entail?

The internal assessment of performing can be organised more flexibly than an assessment requiring a visiting examiner. Individual assessments, for example, can take place in the classroom, during a normal Music period set aside for the purpose. But it is with ensemble performance that the advantages of course-work assessment of performing become fully apparent. Ensembles may arise naturally from the members of a GCSE class, but it is more than likely that at least one candidate will wish to be assessed as a member of a group which is not part of the GCSE class, or even the school. Let us take two very different examples. A pupil may be organist at a local church, and take some part in rehearsing and directing the choir. An assessment of his work in this field would necessitate the teacher visiting the pupil at the church itself, where the music would be made in an appropriate atmosphere and acoustic. Another may play in a steel band at a youth centre, and a visit there would enable the teacher to hear how the pupil functions within the chosen ensemble, making music in conditions that are more relaxed and less formal than in school.

Pupils who are used to external assessment through participation in grade examinations will need careful explanation of the nature of the performing coursework assessment. Although the final tape sent to the Moderator may be of short duration (only 10–20 minutes), it will be the culmination of a number of periodic assessment sessions held over the two years of the course. Before such sessions, it needs to be made clear to the pupils that the assessor will indeed be the school Music teacher, and the candidate's own instrumental teacher may also be involved. Now that it is central to the course, a substantial amount of time each week can at last be given to performing, particularly ensemble work, during lesson time. There is no reason why periodic assessments should not occur in lesson time, resulting naturally from the routine performing activity.

There are three possible levels of assessment.

- *Informal*: Such as may occur in every lesson, where assessments are given verbally, or in the form of brief comments at the end of a piece of written work (such as a score for a composition). It is during informal assessments that learning processes can be observed. The most important aspect of *practice* is the development of musical self-awareness, of the art of listening to oneself.
- *Formal*: More structured periodic assessments, with tape recording, which may act as a rehearsal for the moderation assessment, or indeed for the final 'recital' if the assessment is to be external. For such sessions, teachers may wish to use copies of the assessment forms supplied by the Examination Group, if such forms are available.
- *Final*: The eventual polished presentation for moderation purposes. For this the use of Group assessment forms, if available, will be essential. Many of these allow space for an overall account of the pupil's progress.

What performing styles are open to assessment?

The Criteria state that:

> 3. an enormous range of technical attainment and musical styles is anticipated in the composing and performing sections, and in both of these the widest possible canvas should be available.

They remind us that the GCSE Music examination is not just designed to cater for those pupils who are advantaged through lessons in established peripatetic tuition schemes. There are others able to excel in their own field and in their own styles of performing.

Whereas the Criteria specify a number of points concerning the assessment of composing, they do not go into detail about the assessment of performing, although they do seem to identify two broad categories of performance. One is the more 'traditional' or 'classical' mode of performing whose starting point is the realisation of a score. A performance of a solo piano piece for a grade examination or of a second cornet part in a brass quintet would be examples of this. The other category is performance largely learnt by ear, either from live performance, or, as is more likely these days, recordings. Folk, jazz, rock and other traditions that tend to be passed on aurally are generally learnt in this way.

What are the criteria for the assessment of a performance which involves the realisation of a score?

Most syllabuses are not very explicit about this, concentrating instead on relating a set of broad assessment criteria to a marking scheme. However, the LEAG does go into greater detail about the assessment of performing, and because of this it is worth referring to, even by teachers working to other syllabuses. The LEAG first of all gives, like the other Groups, some broad criteria which apply to all performance:

> *ACCURACY* in playing or singing from notation (whatever form of notation is used)
> *MUSICALITY*: to include
> phrasing
> tempo
> expression
> dynamics
> quality of tone
> *PRESENTATION*: to include rapport with the listener
> *UNDERSTANDING* of the nature and style of the music performed
>
> from LEAG syllabus, p. 8

It then details performance criteria specific to each instrumental group, namely keyboards, strings, woodwind, brass, percussion, electronic instruments, plucked strings and voice. Here are the criteria for brass:

> *Brass*
> Phrasing, interpretation and style
> Tone control
> Intonation
> Embouchure
> Correct breathing and breath control
> Articulation
> Appropriate finger or slide technique
> Hand/bell technique for horn players
> Posture
> Pitch range
> Dynamic range
>
> from LEAG syllabus, p. 10

Activity 11

Using the above as a guide, make a verbal assessment of the two brass performances on the accompanying tape (Examples 1b and 1c). Do not give numerical marks or grades. Example 1c is presented in two takes. What differences do you observe between them? What evidence is there of a process of self-criticism here?

Activity 12

Without consulting what the LEAG syllabus suggests about keyboard instruments, make your own list of criteria that you would apply to the assessment of *piano playing*.

Now apply these criteria to a verbal assessment of the two solo piano performances (Examples 1a and 1e).

Activity 13

Now devise criteria for *strings*, and make an assessment of the accompanied 'cello performance (Example 1d).

What are the criteria for assessing a performance in a style which is less dependent upon the realisation of a score?

The Criteria state:

> 6.3.3 In traditional styles of music associated with piano, voice, orchestral and brass band instruments, it will be assumed that the interpretive skills and technical demands will be approximately equal to those of the GCE/CSE system. (For example, a prepared performance gaining very high marks would be one that would also gain a distinction to the Grade 5 practical examinations of the graded examination boards.) In more modern styles of music which are associated, for example, with Afro-Caribbean or folk music, it is expected that traditional methods of assessment which lay emphasis on the realisation of a score are less helpful. Nevertheless, the demands of such music in terms of interpretive and technical skills are comparable with traditional forms of music making.

It is a little ironic to read of 'folk music', or Afro-Caribbean music for that matter, being described as being associated with 'more modern styles'. In reality the only modern aspect is not the styles, some of which have been around rather longer than either brass bands or grade examinations, but the educational thinking which has belatedly accepted them as valid and legitimate musical activities which pupils can take pleasure in and learn from. However, if these less 'traditional' styles are to be accommodated and accepted into a GCSE scheme, there will need to be a widening of the range of performing criteria.

In the Examples, there are a number of performances by pupils working in 'Afro-American' styles, that is styles related to jazz or pop music. In all cases, there is something given – that is, the pupils concerned are performing a song or improvising over a fixed chord progression. The main differences are that what is given is not notated but has been picked up by ear, and that there is frequently an element of improvisation in the performance. As has been remarked in Part 1, improvisation occurs most naturally here in the context of a *prepared* performance – an instrumental 'break' in the middle of a known pop song, or a singer's own vocal ornamentations on the original melody of the song itself. Improvisations need not be elaborate, and in many cases may consist of the simplest additions or alterations to the given material. Although the non-classical styles exemplified in the Examples relate to pop and jazz, they share performing characteristics with other non-western cultures.

The following features may be worth considering in making assessments.

- *Rhythm*: A feeling for 'swing' and syncopation against a strong, steady beat. There is often a sense of playfulness in the way jazz and rock performers reconcile the opposites of great rhythmic flexibility with a rock-solid rhythmic foundation, often to the extent of being consistently behind or in front of the pulse.
- *Pitch*: Performers in these styles frequently start notes slightly off-pitch, or 'bend' the pitch of notes that are sustained. The technical term for this is 'nuance', more commonly known as 'blue notes'. This effect is only rarely used in classical performance (where it is known as *portamento*), and can be disconcerting at first if one is familiar with notes being pitched 'right in the centre'. However, 'nuance' is the lifeblood not only of jazz and rock performing, but also of many other non-western styles, such as Indian music. In addition to this, singers and wind players may cultivate a much wider vibrato than is acceptable in classical performance.
- *Tone*: Classical singing and playing aims for a rounded, pure sound, with a well controlled vibrato. The sounds of many jazz and rock instrumentalists may at first seem coarse in comparison. A well known example would be to compare the sound of Billie Holiday's voice with that of an opera singer. But we need to ask: is the vocal or instrumental sound being produced *expressive in its context*, even if it does not conform to the norms of *bel canto*?
- *Articulation and phrasing, dynamics*: Good performers in these styles will be as sensitive to these aspects as will their counterparts in classical performing.

Activity 14

Although improvisation plays only a small, and optional, part in the final assessment for GCSE, it can play a most useful role in the composing process. Composition, it has been said, is akin to 'slowed-down improvisation', and improvisation, being the articulation of thoughts that immediately spring to mind, is akin to sketching for a composition. Some improvisations featured in the Examples are presented in two different 'takes', enabling the process of invention to be heard as it unfolds.

Listen to recorded Examples 3a–3d, of pupils improvising on a 12-bar blues pattern. Make verbal assessments indicating the *feeling* for style indicated by these recordings. Pay particular attention to aspects such as swing and syncopation, blue notes (how does the pianist in Example 3c convey this aspect of the style?), use of vibrato, articulation, dynamics and tone quality.

Listen again to the two successive bass xylophone improvisations made by the same pupil on the blues pattern in Example 3a. Notice the way (a) a unifying idea emerges during the first improvisation, and (b) this idea is developed in the second. Which of the two improvisations is more successful? Why?

Activity 15

A variety of singing styles is encompassed in the Examples: folk (2d), pop/blues (3b, 5b(iii), 9c and 10a), and classical (10b). List (a) the criteria which you think should apply to all singing, whatever the style, and (b) the criteria which apply specially to the non-classical styles exemplified. Make a brief assessment of the folk song performance, 'Stewball', Example 2d, enumerating the strengths of the performance and also those aspects which could be improved.

What criteria are applicable to ensemble performance?

There are criteria which are especially relevant to ensemble performing, which should be considered alongside those for individual performing, when a pupil is being assessed either as a member or as a director of a group or a band. These will include sensitive balance and blending of dynamics, agreement about phrasing and ensemble coordination. Where non-classical styles are concerned, skills such as collective improvising should also be considered. For example, players in a jazz or rock group may pick up and develop ideas originally improvised by others.

The NISEC syllabus gives a thorough and detailed list of criteria for rehearsing and directing an ensemble, including:

- planning and choice of material
- ability to detect errors and work on them effectively
- discipline and leadership qualities
- ability to communicate and sustain the group's attention
- the ability to realise the composer's musical intentions.

paraphrased from NISEC syllabus, pp. 7–8

Activity 16

Make brief assessments of the *individual* contributions made to the examples of ensemble performance recorded in the classroom (Examples 1d, 2a and 2b). Concentrate in particular upon the following individuals:
(a) the 'cellist and pianist in Example 1d;
(b) the flute and bass xylophone players in Example 2a;
(c) the oboe, bass guitar and saxophone in Example 2b.

Activity 17

Make an assessment of the reggae duet (recorded Example 2c). This is an example of collective improvising, involving two performers.

1 What differences of approach are there in the second take?
2 Is there any evidence that the two players are listening to each other?

How is performing assessment converted into a mark?

Music is not a subject where there are right or wrong answers. Assessment is complex, and initially words have to be used to describe the experience of listening to a candidate's performance. Only then is the examiner in a position to convert the assessment into a mark. The Criteria give a number of 'grade descriptions', and each syllabus gives approximate mark descriptions. Here is an example of a mark description scheme for individual performing:

Mark

1 Attempts to perform
2 Gives a weak performance with little knowledge of appropriate pitch and/or rhythm and expression
3 Gives a weak performance with some control and an attempt at interpretation of the music
4 Gives a rather weak performance with some control and an attempt at interpretation of the music
5 Gives a fair performance with some control and an attempt at interpretation of the music with occasional success
6 Gives a fair performance in which fluency is occasionally lost with consequent lack of expression
7 A fluent performance with good control of the medium but lacking phrasing or expression
8 A fluent performance with only very minor slips as regards phrasing and expression
9 A very good performance which is technically able and musical, only lacking in total commitment
10 An outstanding performance which is accurate, imaginative and convincing

from MEG (B) syllabus, p. 32

Another factor to be considered is the *level of difficulty* of the performance. The Criteria stipulate that:

> 6.3.2 tests of performance will automatically provide a differentiated form of assessment since candidates will be guided by their teachers as to the standard of technical difficulty and interpretive demands of the music they offer. It will, therefore, be necessary to draw up schemes of assessment which will take into account both the difficulty of the music and the standard of performance.

In grade practical examinations the level of difficulty has already been decided by the Board prescribing the pieces set for performance, and indicated by the actual grade (I–VIII). The mark out of 150 indicates the candidate's level of attainment *within that particular grade*. With GCSE, it is the teacher who must give guidance to candidates and their parents as to the level of difficulty and the way it affects the mark given. For candidates entered for grade examinations, there already is a yardstick, indicated by the Criteria: that a performance gaining a 'distinction' in Grade V would also be one that gained high marks at GCSE. But care and tact must be exercised in conveying the likely performance outcome to pupils who do not have the benefit of this external yardstick of performance. Such pupils would be those who are near-beginners on their instruments, those whose experience of music-making has been entirely within the classroom, and those who play instruments or work in styles other than those covered by the grade examination boards. The Criteria require marking schemes to combine level of difficulty with level of attainment, for, where Music is concerned, one can find beginners and experienced performers in almost any age group. Someone who has been learning the violin since the age of seven will clearly be able to take on a more demanding challenge than someone who only started learning an instrument at the beginning of the GCSE course.

The policy of most Examining Groups is to make use of a 'difficulty multiplier'. This means that the candidate is given a mark (say, out of 10, as with MEG (B)) for the quality of the performance, and then to multiply it by a figure reflecting the level of difficulty of the performing task:

> For very easy pieces of music the multiplier is 1. For pieces and tasks of intermediate difficulty the multiplier is 2 and for music and tasks of reasonable difficulty (appropriate to candidates whose skills are of a standard which would have attracted GCE grades A-C) the multiplier is 3.
>
> A candidate with a very good performance on a piece of intermediate difficulty thus scores 9 x 2 = 18 marks. The score could also be obtained by a candidate with a fair performance on a piece of reasonable difficulty.
>
> from MEG (B) syllabus, p. 31

This syllabus also supplies criteria for the difficulty multiplier:

> *Very easy* (multiplier 1): hymn line, folk style or march; repetitive; short (8-16 bars); requiring minimal control of medium and limited interpretive insight.
>
> *Intermediate difficulty* (multiplier 2): more extended structure; requiring some measure of technical competence and interpretive insight.
>
> *Reasonable difficulty* (multiplier 3): typically requiring secure control and mature understanding of style.
>
> from MEG (B) syllabus, p. 31

The maximum mark (for an oustanding performance of a piece of reasonable difficulty) would therefore be 30, according to the MEG (B) scheme.

The following table gives the marking schemes for performing followed by the different examining groups.

Group	*Mark out of*	*Difficulty multiplier*	*Maximum obtainable*
LEAG	12	none	12
MEG (A)	20	1, 1½, 2, 2½, 3	60
MEG ((B)	10	1 2, 3	30
NEA	12	1, 1½, 2	24
SEG	a more complex scheme involving a graph: refer to syllabus, pp. 63-5		40
WJEC	12	1, 1½, 2, 2½, 3	36
NISEC	13½	1, 2, 3	40½

Activity 18

Using either the MEG (B) difficulty indicators referred to above, or those of your own Group syllabus, make an estimate of the *level of difficulty* of the pieces performed in recorded Examples 1a to 1e (individual performances). Give a numerical figure to indicate the level of difficulty.

Now, on the basis of the verbal appraisals made previously (Activities 11 to 13), give a *mark for attainment* (out of 10 for MEG (B)) and multiply this by your difficulty indicator to give a final mark (out of 30 for MEG (B)).

Activity 19

Carry out a similar exercise on the recorded examples of ensemble performing (Examples 2a–2d), with reference to the following individuals:

(a) the flute and bass xylophone in 2a;
(b) the oboe, bass guitar and saxophone in 2b;
(c) the drummer in 2c (make your difficulty indicator show what you estimate to be this drummer's level of technical ability);
(d) the two singers in 2d (assess the singing only).

---

3 Assessing composing

What does the assessment of composing entail?

Released from the tyranny of final, timed examination papers, coursework assessment need no longer be concerned solely with end-products. Teachers can now convey in their assessments something of what a pupil has gained in skill, knowledge and understanding through composing or performing. Where a pupil's composition is concerned, we can now ask not only 'What does it sound like?', or 'Does it make musical sense?', but also 'What developments in the pupil's skill, imagination and understanding have come about through the act of making this piece?' In the assessment of composing, as with performing, bald numerical marks are insufficient. Teachers will need to develop skills for assessing composing work, to enable the writing of assessments that are brief and to the point, and to convey the nature of the achievement in musical terms. But composing assessments will also need to convey something of the way pupils have come to terms with the processes of generating ideas, developing them, and shaping them into some kind of coherent whole.

The reader is strongly recommended to study the paper 'Examinations and assessment' by Richard Orton, which appears as Appendix II to John Paynter's *Music in the Secondary School Curriculum* (1982, pp. 215–20). Not only is this a clear and stimulating article, setting out the complex range of variables that feature in a composition, but it has had considerable influence on the Criteria, and, through the Criteria, the Group syllabuses.

Orton sees composition as the balancing of opposing tendencies – the control of variety in relation to the urge for unity, and the shaping of a piece of music in relation to its timespan. 'Control of variety' refers to the content, and 'unity' to the style and organisation of the piece. Orton is concerned also with assessing the process, the 'involvement' of composers with their material, whether 'given' or 'chosen'.

It can be easy sometimes to confuse process with product. Take the word 'experimental', for example. This is how it is used when the Criteria enumerate the various elements to be considered when assessing compositions:

> 6.4.4.1 Variety: rhythm, duration and tempo, pitch, melody and harmony.
> In experimental work these may be replaced by density, articulation, timbre, nuance and location.

The word 'experimental' here seems to allude to certain received styles of contemporary music rather than to the actual *process* of experiment. But there is a world of difference between what an adult, musically sophisticated composer, and a child may regard as 'experimental'. Pieces which explore diatonic tonality, such as the piano duet, Example 6, may be just as experimental *for the pupils concerned* as those whose explorations take them closer to the pre-occupations of the *avant garde*, such as the sonorities which may be obtained from an old piano frame (Example 4c). Both are experiments, not because they 'sound experimental', but because children are learning things that are *new to them* about the materials of sound through the processes involved. By the use of the expression 'these may be replaced by . . .', the Criteria seem also to imply that other styles of composing, involving more conventional emphases such as rhythm, melody and harmony, are less experimental.

Indeed all creative arts activity is concerned not only with balancing unity with variety, but also with the relationship within variety of the familiar and the unfamiliar. A teacher must understand the needs many pupils have to use the known as a starting point for their explorations into the new and unknown. There is no reason, therefore, why pastiche cannot also be experimental. The two songs, Examples 10a and 10b, are strongly influenced by stylistic models, although both contain turns of phrase and choices of chord that are personal to the composers, indicating directions in which they are likely to develop. Again, these are experiments for the pupils concerned, even though the style of one of the songs could hardly be called 'contemporary':

> This is a perfectly natural and musical process. It is one of the ways in which styles develop. If we are to grow as composers we need to assimilate and 'to make our own', stylistic features which we glean from the work of others – especially where those features seem to have a particular meaning for us and are aligned with our own attempts at musical expression.
>
> John Paynter, 1982, p. 120

The assessment of the musical achievement, and the recording of the learning process, then, need to go hand in hand. One of the most satisfying experiences for a creative arts teacher is to observe the process of development in a pupil where an individual style gradually emerges. There are some tantalising glimpses of individuality in the two songs mentioned above, and we can learn a great deal from observing how originality emerged in some well known and well documented cases. For example, we can witness the creative process at work if we get to know the musical development of some of the great composers. In all introspective accounts by composers of their work, it is the *powers of self-criticism* which are crucial to the composing process. 'What has been set down in a moment of ardour must now be critically examined, improved, extended or condensed as the form requires', wrote Tchaikowsky, a composer whose Romantic style belied his disciplined and painstaking method of working. The best known documentation of creative self-criticism can be found in the sketches of Beethoven, showing the evolution of fully fledged, shapely and distinctive themes from relatively banal beginnings. The overall process of Beethoven's stylistic development also tells a fascinating story. Compare, for example, the openings of his two piano sonatas in the key of F minor. Both start with a tonic arpeggio figure. In the early sonata, Op. 2, the arpeggio is almost a cliché of the late eighteenth century style, having none of the weight and personality of the opening of the *Appassionata* sonata, Op. 57. What process has brought about this transformation in composing approach and technique? In the years that intervened between the early sonata and the *Appassionata*, the intellectually curious and imaginative mind of Beethoven took him on a journey away from the polite stylistic norms of his youth to a thorough-going exploration of the materials of sound and their expressive powers. The hollow sound of the hands playing two octaves apart, the telling silences between the phrases, the greater harmonic daring, and the subtle rhythmic notation, are all evidence of a composer who has learnt from his craft and has matured inwardly. He has also learnt to compose music uniquely characteristic of the medium for which he is writing. The early piece could be played on a variety of instruments – a string quartet, or a harpsichord even. But the *Appassionata* would sound convincing only on a piano.

The process of development from imitation of an admired model towards a more individual style is reflected in the careers of many creative musical artists.

Take the example of a very different musician from another era, the great jazz saxophonist Charlie Parker, here reminiscing on the emergence of his own unique improvising style:

> I'd been getting bored with the stereotyped changes that were being used all the time at the time, and I kept thinking there's bound to be something else. I could hear it sometimes, but I couldn't play it.
>
> Well, that night, I was working over *Cherokee*, and, as I did, I found that by using the higher intervals of a chord as a melody line and backing them with appropriately related changes, I could play the thing I'd been hearing. I came alive.
>
> Quoted in Shapiro & Hentoff, 1955, p. 354

The above is a description of one of the most outstandingly successful creative experiments in twentieth century music. Parker's 'coming alive' was the result of insight rooted again in self-criticism. Another jazz musician, speaking in interview, gives us an insight into the way the act of creation was shared among members of his band having an entire sound pallette available for the immediate testing of ideas.

> 'When we're all working together, a guy may have an idea and he plays it in his horn. Another guy may add to it and make something out of it. Someone may play a riff and ask, 'How do you like this?' The trumpets may try something together and say, 'Listen to this'. There may be a difference of opinion on what kind of mute to use. Someone may advocate extending a note or cutting it off. The sax section may want to put an additional smear on it.'
>
> Duke Ellington,
> from Shapiro & Hentoff, 1955, p. 225

It is insights and experiments, enabling the growth of skill, understanding and imagination, that we need to observe when assessing the development of children's work. (For accounts of the development of individual pupils' composing work, see Spencer 1980, pp. 113–121, and Bunting 1987, pp. 25–52.)

How does one assess the composing process?

In common with all other GCSE subjects, one of the intentions behind the upgrading of coursework is to enable a focus on the learning process. However, only two of the Groups, the SEG and the MEG, make a convincing attempt in their syllabuses to incorporate process into the composing criteria, or to give guidance about its appraisal. The MEG (B) syllabus is helpfully explicit about the teacher's responsibility for supervising composing coursework, both to enable documentation of the process, and to ensure authentication:

> Although the precise means of maintaining supervision will inevitably differ from centre to centre and with the type of work chosen, it is expected that the teacher will be involved at the following stages.
>
> (a) Initial discussion at the time when the theme is chosen and the work is being planned. The teacher must be involved in the choice of theme and must make notes on the discussion.
> (b) Discussion, either initially or in the early stages, of the availability and use of source material and method of presentation.
> (c) Periodic supervision and discussion of each composition including making notes of the discussion.
> (d) Discussion at any time when composing is completed to resolve any doubts about the work that has been presented. The teacher must make notes on the discussion.
> (e) Guidance on presentation of the compositions.
> (f) Certification by the teacher that the marks shown were awarded in accordance with the Group's Instructions.
>
> from MEG (B) syllabus, p. 35

Activity 20

1 Listen closely to the piano duet, Example 6, *without reading the annotation made by the pupil.* Make an assessment of the piece as an end-product. Does the piece strike a satisfactory balance between unity and variety? The piece is in ternary form. Listen particularly closely to the middle section. What grasp of musical processes does this show?

2 Now read the annotation made by one of the pupils who composed the piece. The Criteria for the listening component (3.1.1) require candidates to 'respond to the structural and expressive elements of music using technical and/or non-technical language'. How well does this pupil reveal her understanding of the structural and expressive elements of her own piece in this annotation, which also uses 'technical and non-technical language'? What does she reveal about her own composing process and her powers of self-appraisal?

The reader's attention is drawn in particular to the following phrases used by the pupil in her annotation:

'It was decided early on, that the piece should concentrate particularly on "echoes".'

'Although the piece sounds rather "simple", it took a fair time to complete.'

'An unusual sound – one major set of notes being played with a set of minor notes.'

'I played a B major arpeggio . . . and gradually this turned minor.'

Will the assessment of melody writing and harmony within the tonal system be any different from O-level?

Although the Criteria state (6.4.3) that 'Assessment of written techniques within the tonal system should not prove to be too difficult since reliable and proven methods of assessment have been used by GCE and CSE Boards for many years', there are a number of points to bear in mind as a result of the much wider canvas of styles admitted. The first point is that while many pupil compositions will make use of techniques within the tonal system, not all of these will be *written*. The second is that melody-writing and harmony exercises in O-level and CSE papers allowed scope for a very restricted kind of tonality, and disregarded twentieth century developments such as bi-tonality and the use of scales other than major or minor. Of the recorded examples, under a half make use of diatonic tonality in a way that would be expected at O-level, and most of these, by virtue of their being extended pieces of coursework rather than short exercises in a timed paper, are able to use a much wider harmonic vocabulary giving candidates scope to demonstrate an understanding of tonality's expressive power.

None of the other examples of composition explores tonality in the limited O-level sense of being either in a major or minor mode, or implying functional harmonies. Some of the group classroom pieces in Examples 4 and 5 exploit melodic lines and accompaniment figures derived from the pentatonic scale, or when they do use the diatonic scale, build static layered textures out of repeated figures, so that the effect, to use Orton's words, is 'modal, rather than functional, giving a sense of timelessness' (1982, p. 218). The arrangement of 'God rest you merry, gentlemen' (Example 5c) derives all its harmonies and ostinato figurations from the Aeolian mode of the original. It is in the form of two variations, contrasted in metre and tempo, which entertainingly establish a kinship between the disparate musical worlds of the English folk carol (the source material), and the pop and jazz styles of its two variations. The composer/arranger is making use of musical influences that appeal to her, and in so doing is showing an intuitive flair for composing techniques.

Activity 21

Listen to the two pieces composed by the same pupil, Examples 7a and 7b. They are presented in order of composition. About the first piece, the rondo for solo flute, the pupil's GCSE teacher commented: 'In my first term we concentrate on "one line" music hence this composition, though he has written piano music as well. However, I think that this is a worthwhile example of his work, quite well worked out, and with an interesting melodic line.'

1 Comment on the way both pieces achieve (a) unity, and (b) variety.
2 Compare the way tonality is used in both pieces.
3 Are there any musical preoccupations in the first piece which are carried over and developed in the second? What aspects of composing skill and musical understanding are being grasped and developed here?

Activity 22

Now study the way both pieces have been notated by the composer. How effective are the two scores as pieces of communication to a prospective performer? The pupil's teacher suggested he change the G sharps in Example 7a to A flats. Assuming that you agree with this suggestion, how would you have explained the reasons for this to the composer?

What musical influences can you detect in the style of these pieces? Has he been listening to rondos by other composers? What listening would you suggest to him both to reinforce the ideas and musical organising skills developed through composing these pieces, and to stimulate him to compose further?

What elements apart from melody and harmony need to be considered?

Rhythm

Pupils' compositions may show a lively receptivity to the influence of the rhythmic innovations of twentieth century music whether from composers such as Stravinsky and Bartók or from popular music. Children can certainly feel and hear a variety of rhythmic effects, even if many do not have the intellectual means to notate them. All the following effects may be found in the Examples.

Assymetrical metres

Use of time-signatures outside the common-or-garden world of 3/4, 4/4 or 6/8. Metres such as 5/4 (Examples 5c and 7a).

Cross rhythms

One of the commonest cross rhythms, frequently used in baroque music, is the *hemiola*, the imposition of 2/4 over an established 3/4 metre. Another, more dramatic version of this effect is to alternate between compound and simple time. A well known modern example of this is the song 'America' from Bernstein's *West Side Story*, but the effect can also be found in Monteverdi. Gentle cross-rhythms exploiting the ambiguities latent in 6/4 time are exploited to good effect in the piano piece 'Sunrise', Example 9a, although the rhythmic inventiveness creates problems for the pupil in notating her piece.

Additive rhythms

These are metrical patterns made up of unequal units. The layered ostinato accompaniment to the second of the 'Swing low' arrangements (Example 5b) uses one of the commonest of these, the calypso, splitting an 8/8 bar into groups of 3 + 3 + 2 quavers. Well known examples of additive rhythms in the repertoire can be found in the song 'Jamaica Farewell', the Dances in Bulgarian Rhythm from Bartók's *Mikrokosmos, Book VI*, and the guitar introduction to Chuck Berry's rock'n'roll number, 'Johnny B. Goode'.

Syncopation

This effect, common in classical music, is part of the lifeblood of the jazz-derived styles of Afro-American popular music. But whereas the syncopation in classical music is *composed*, syncopation in jazz and popular-derived styles is often inserted by the performer as part of the improvisation. One common performing practice is for a main singer or instrumentalist to play around with the established beat, sometimes slipping behind or ahead of the main pulse for a whole phrase at a time. The singer/arranger of Example 5c can be heard doing this in her opening slow tempo variation on the carol. In styles outside the western tradition, the transition between performing and composing is often no more clear-cut than the transition between night and day.

Pitch

The topic of pitch is not exhausted by considerations of 'traditional' melody and harmony, and extensions such as exotic scales and modes. Other aspects which appear in pupils' work, which, like rhythm, show the influence of both popular and 'serious' contemporary styles, include: bitonality, chromaticism, nuance and non-functional harmonic effects such as chord clusters.

Bitonality

This is a device common in twentieth century music, where two keys are implied simultaneously. It can be heard in the opening section of Stravinsky's *Rite of Spring*, for example. The use of bitonality in the layered texture of Example 4a has been mentioned previously, and the effect also occurs in Example 9a, in bars 25–7.

Chromaticism

The use of melodic figures and chords outside the scale or mode on which the piece is based is again common. In Example 3d, the guitarist uses a number of altered chords, and in Example 9c a highly chromatic ostinato forms the basis of a piece where the tonal centre is only weakly discernible. By giving it the title 'Infinity', the composer helps the listener to focus on the expressive intention of her piece.

Nuance

This term refers to slight variations in pitch found, for example, in electronic music. However, their most well known usage is to be found in the 'blue notes' of jazz and rock performers. In these styles they most frequently take the form of flat thirds or sevenths in the context of a major tonality, often creating 'false relations' with the accompaniment and bass line, which retain the sharp third and leading note. As with syncopation, it is often difficult to tell whether nuances are composed or improvised spontaneously in performance. Both blue notes and syncopation feature in the vocal line of Example 10a, the song, 'I was wrong.'

Non-functional harmonic effects

This approach to chords as sonorities interesting in themselves rather than functional harmonies contributing to the unfolding musical argument was first initiated in the West by composers like Debussy. It is not surprising that pupils in their teens will wish to explore chords purely for the sheer sensual pleasure of their sound. In Example 10a, a song heavily influenced by pop and rock styles, the piano part occasionally uses chord clusters, an effect quite outside the normal vocabulary of the idiom. By using a sound she has discovered for herself rather than imitated from other music, the pupil is beginning to show signs of individuality.

Density, dynamics, articulation, timbre and location

These elements are traditionally subsidiary to pitch and rhythm, but they are present in all kinds of music. Because they are less amenable to precise notation, their assessment will have to be made by ear rather than by studying scores.

Density

The term refers to texture. Extremes of density might be represented at one end by Tallis's 40-part motet, *Spem in alium*, and at the other by Debussy's *Syrinx* for solo flute. Contrasts in density can have great dramatic power. The slow introduction to Stravinsky's *Rite of Spring*, for example, builds up an extremely complex texture, and the section which follows, the 'Dance of the adolescents' with its famous irregular accentuation, derives much of its power from being relatively sparse in contrast.

Textures may consist of a number of layers performing different functions – for example a vocal melody with an arpeggiated accompaniment, a melody over a layered texture of ostinatos, or a contrapuntal texture made up of independent or inter-related melodic lines.

Dynamics

Dynamics markings are noticeably absent from the scores in Part 2. However, they are far from absent from many of the performances on the recordings, whether scored or unscored. Dynamic shadings feature in the improvisations of Example 3, and in several of the compositions. Recording 4b, a group composition, has a well controlled *diminuendo* at the end (spoiled in the recording by a disturbance in the lesson where this was recorded). The piano introduction to Example 10a, the song 'I was wrong', is played by its composer with an expressive ebb and flow of volume.

Articulation and timbre

These can be as important in the musical content as pitch and rhythm. The following comes from one of Tchaikowsky's letters:

> 'I invent the musical idea and the instrumentation simultaneously. Thus I thought out the scherzo of our symphony – at the moment of its composition – exactly as you heard it. In is inconceivable except as *pizzicato*. Were it played with the bow, it would lose all its charm and be a mere body without a soul.'
>
> from R. Newmarch (ed.), 1906, pp. 280–1

Once music is being created *as sound* in the classroom, and not on paper as an abstraction which most pupils cannot hear anyway, timbre becomes an exciting consideration. Many contemporary idioms place timbre, articulation and the exploration of textural density uppermost in the hierarchy of musical materials: this is certainly true of certain pieces by Ligeti and Penderecki. The two lower-school pieces heard in Example 4c explore tone colours and modes of attack possible with sounds from single sources – a cymbal and an old piano frame. Despite the absence of pitch as an organising element, both indicate a strong tendency to create clear and simple rhythmic patterns. The second piece is also in a tightly organised ABA form.

Timbre does not play such a prominent or variegated role in the individually composed Examples, but it is an important presence nevertheless. There is a feeling for delicate, almost impressionistic piano-writing in Example 9a, 'Sunrise', both in the composing and in the execution of the piece on the recording.

Timbre and articulation also feature importantly in non-classical music. The four blues recordings, again, show an awareness of these two aspects, particularly 3b and 3d, the latter revealing a variety of colouristic guitar effects, from harmonics to the sound of fingers scratching the strings at the very end.

Location

Location is concerned with the positioning of sound in space. It has been a preoccupation of composers since the late Renaissance, and of course features in the dramatic choral exchanges in Bach's *St Matthew Passion*. With modern studio techniques, location has become an important feature of the work of electronic composers and recording producers. It is certainly an important feature of the process of making rock LPs.

Activity 23

Make a written appraisal of the piece for flute and clarinet, Example 8, in the light of the teacher's own annotation about the origins of the piece:

> 'The duet for flute and clarinet was the result of looking at a Bach two-part invention, particularly from the point of view of rhythmic counterpoint. The work on it was assiduous, and the way it ultimately completely diverged from the original model shows that it was also unaided.'

1. Compare bars 1–17 with bars 18–33. Both sections use the same material, but differ in subtle and interesting ways. What do they tell you about the composers' harmonic ear, their imagination, their powers of organisation?
2. Silence is a recurring element in the piece. Are the silences effective, and if so, why?
3. The score lacks tempo indications, or markings of dynamics and articulation. Does the composers' performance do justice to the score? Does their score do justice to the performance?
4. The rhythm in bars 38ff is inaccurately notated. How has this inaccuracy arisen? If the composers had given tempo indications that reflected the way the piece is performed, could this inaccuracy have been avoided?

How does one convert a composing assessment into a mark?

The Examining Groups vary considerably in their approaches to converting composing assessments into marks, just as they vary in the degree of advice given about the assessment of composing. One approach is to give a 'mark description', as with performing, and to indicate a range of marks that tallies with that description. This is the approach adopted by both NEA and WJEC in their syllabuses Here is the NEA's description of their lowest range of marks, out of a total of 30.

> 0–10 Compositions in this category will display a basic understanding of the demands of composition.
> At the top of the scale candidates might be expected to invent or select a musical idea of the order of simple folk tunes or nursery rhymes and present a simple arrangement of them with very basic chords and/or percussion accompaniment of moderate rhythmic interest.
> The lower end of the scale will contain candidates for whom any form of composing or arranging is difficult.
>
> from NEA syllabus, p. 25

The LEAG and NISEC adopt a different approach, linking their marking schemes to a choice of criteria suited to an individual composition. The LEAG, in particular, is thorough and explicit:

> Each piece is marked out of 100, apportioned as follows.
>
> *30 marks* are available for award according to the following criteria:
> (a) degree to which the candidate maintains the chosen style;
> (b) fluency and success with which the candidate exploits the material and medium;
> (c) impact and overall impression of the work.
>
> *70 marks* are available for award according to the criteria chosen by the examiner as most appropriate to each piece. Each criterion selected is to be weighted (10, 20 or 30 marks). Examiners should use a minimum of three and a maximum of five criteria.
>
> (d) Form: structure, balance, scale, repetition/contrast, development of musical ideas, climax.
>
> (e) Medium: use of instruments/voices/sound sources, and understanding of their capabilities; clarity and contrast.
>
> (f) Notation: accuracy and consistency within the chosen system. Does the notation adequately represent the desired sound? Can it be performed?
>
> (g) Melody: degree to which the melody satisfies the aim. Flow, contour, ornamentation, phrase length and shape, repetition, sequence, scale shapes, implied harmony.
>
> (h) Harmony/Accompaniment: appropriateness of chosen style.
>
> (i) Tempo/Rhythm: relationship between tempo and rhythm, metre, cross-rhythms.
>
> (j) Texture: layering, counterpoint, manipulation of density.
>
> (k) Location: spatial separation of instruments or loudspeakers in electronic music and musique concrète.
>
> (l) Dynamics: appropriate use and control, balance.
>
> from LEAG syllabus, pp. 11–12

By allowing assessors to select a range of criteria, positive achievements can be more fairly indentified. No candidate need be penalised for failing to achieve what he or she did not set out to do in the first place. It also takes care of the thorny question of notation. Notation need only be assessed where it is appropriate to the piece concerned. The flexible weightings also ensure that if notation has to be considered and is found to be weak in accuracy, it can be given a lower weighting against the more positive aspects of a piece, such as imaginative content and clear organisation.

Accuracy of notation, on the other hand, can receive full recognition where appropriate. A score that is a genuinely effective piece of musical communication, and matches well its realisation in performance, may be rewarded as a positive achievement by being given a high mark within a more generous weighting.

Activity 24

Listen to, and follow the score of Example 9a, the piano piece 'Sunrise'. Using the LEAG system of optional criteria given above, decide which criteria you would choose in order to asses the piece, and which weightings you would give to each criterion selected. (Remember: 10, 20 or 30 combined to a total of 70; you are allowed a minimum of three and a maximum of five criteria.)

Is the level of difficulty of a particular composing challenge a factor in the assessment, as with performing?

Since the publication of their 1988 syllabus, the WJEC has developed a more explicit approach to the task of converting assessments into marks. In a supplementary booklet, the WJEC suggests that the process of assessing composing work should be conceived in two stages: a *formative* assessment, which would take into account the level of the composing challenge for a particular pupil, while a *summative* assessment would be concerned with the quality of a piece as an end-product. The formative assessment, made by the teacher, would predict the likely outcome of a pupil's composing work based on the teacher's knowledge of the pupil's ability. Naturally, more able and experienced candidates would be encouraged to tackle more ambitious composing tasks. To obtain a high grade, a pupil will need to have succeeded in meeting a greater challenge than one who had performed well on an easier one. This system would ensure that the ablest candidates were stretched and rewarded by doing more difficult work, while less able candidates would do less demanding tasks, while still getting satisfaction out of having created their own music. At the end of the course, there would need to be an alignment made between the formative and summative assessments, and, if they failed to tally, some compromise would need to be reached. The process is analogous to the 'difficulty multiplier' used for the assessment of performance (see p. 75).

Activity 25

The three piano pieces, Examples 9a–c, all came from the same GCSE class and were composed during the first term of the course. Their teacher described the nature of the task set as follows:

> 'The starting point for the compositions was "write a melody". I didn't make any stipulations as to instrument, key, length and I found it interesting that they didn't ask.
>
> 'The titles came on completion of the pieces and as yet I have not dealt with the discrepancies between performance and score, regarding the performance as their true intention.'

Using the old O-level 'melody writing' task as a yardstick exemplifying a 'moderately difficult' challenge, assess the level of challenge of each of the composing tasks undertaken in these three pieces. Estimate the challenge as either: very difficult, difficult, moderately difficult, moderately easy or very easy. Give reasons for your estimation.

Activity 26

Now apply this yardstick to your own situation in school. Into which categories of challenge do the composing tasks currently being undertaken by your GCSE pupils fall?

Can a marking scheme integrate all aspects of composing: the process as well as the product?

Of all the Examining Groups, the SEG is the most comprehensive in its marking scheme, covering both process (formative assessments) and product (summative assessments.) Like the WJEC, the SEG addresses itself to the relationship between composing work, and the nature of the original task set. It is worth studying pages 86–7 of the SEG syllabus closely, even if you are working to another Examination Group, as the advice given is both helpful and thorough, and the mark allocation scheme is the only one that succinctly combines elements of both formative and summative assessments.

Activity 27

The two final examples use the same medium, female voice with piano accompaniment, but are the results of two very different routes to musical accomplishment. Although the reader only hears, and in the case of the second song, also sees, end-results, it is fascinating to speculate on the different learning processes that have taken place. They demonstrate the range of styles in which young people can compose fluently. 'I was wrong' is in a rock idiom, whereas 'The Schoolboy' shows a far from superficial appreciation of the nineteenth century idiom Austro-German *lied* tradition. Both songs reflect their respective traditions in other ways. Both words and music of the rock song were composed by the same pupil, who sings and accompanies herself, with a vocal descant added by a friend. The *lied*-influenced song, on the other hand, sets words by someone else, and is performed by two separate people – a *bel canto* singer, with the composer as accompanist.

The GCSE teacher whose pupil composed the Blake setting made the following commentary:

> 'Maud's song resulted from a lesson in setting words. Tasks varying from fitting a rhythm to a choice of poems; to writing a melody; to writing a melody with bass line and chords; or an accompaniment were set to this GCSE group – each according to ability and advancement.
>
> Maud had a little help with basic 4 part harmony, but the song was entirely her own effort – unchanged in any way – when I made one small suggestion she firmly said NO!'

1 Although they are in such different styles, each song makes use of tonal, functional harmony. Comment on how each song uses tonality for expressive effect, using devices such as chromaticism, modulation, pedal points, etc.
2 Comment on the vocal styles of the songs, on the conception of the piano parts, and the way each responds to its text.
3 Comment on the overall organisation of the songs. What have their composers learnt about musical form through the experience of completing them?
4 Although you will not be able to make formative assessments without knowing the pupils, where would you estimate each song comes in your own Group's composition marking scheme?

4 Moderation, grading, feedback

What forms of moderation are available for music?

Any part of an examination which is internally assessed needs to be subject to a process which ensures that the assessments and marks given by teachers are fair, and can stand comparison with parallel pieces of work or sets of marks given elsewhere in other Centres. This process is known as *moderation*. To quote the General Criteria (p. 23):

> *Moderation* is the process of aligning standards between different examinations, different *components* or (most frequently) different centres or teachers responsible for the *assessment* of their own candidates.

There are two kinds of moderation:

> Moderation by inspection, in which the candidates' work (or samples of their work) is inspected and the original assessments adjusted as necessary to bring them into line with the examining body's general standard. . .
>
> 'Statistical moderation, in which the assessments of the work of a group of candidates in one component are compared statistically with the work in other components. The assessments may then be adjusted to bring them into line with agreed standards.
>
> Mobley *et al.*, 1986, p. 86

What are the moderating policies of the individual Examining Groups?

LEAG

Performing is externally assessed by a visiting examiner, so the moderation will probably be statistical (there is no requirement that the candidate's recital be taped, so moderation by inspection cannot apply).

Moderation in *composition* will be by inspection. After receiving mark sheets completed by teachers, the Moderator (known as the 'Assessor') will send for a sample of work from a selection of candidates. A minimum of ten candidates' work will be looked at, and the sample should cover the whole ability range within the group of candidates. Further background detail about the circumstances of the composition work may be requested.

The LEAG also allows for those teachers who feel that they are not qualified to give an assessment of composing work, by requiring the Assessor to mark the work of candidates not assessed in the first instance by their teachers. (There is some doubt here as to whether composing will, strictly speaking, count as 'coursework' here when this happens.)

SEG

It is the policy of SEG overall to carry out moderation by inspection. Each year, in January, a standardisation process making use of taped examples for assessment drawn from work in previous years will be disseminated to all Music teachers involved in teaching the GCSE. A team of visiting Moderators will visit all areas covered by the Board, and where practicable, groups of teachers together with the GCSE Moderator will meet to make joint assessments of samples of work drawn from the Centres involved. In general, joint assessment sessions are to be encouraged, particularly of performing work. (See p. 89 of syllabus.) The Moderator will also act as joint examiner with the teacher for the *performing* assessments, thus making the Southern Group's performing assessment rather more formal than the internal performing assessments envisaged by some other Examining Groups. The SEG will make available to teachers a training package of examples of compositions representing the full range of ability. Comments on these compositions and details of the marking will be included to enable teachers to use these as standardisation material.

MEG

The moderation process for both *performing* and *composing* will begin initially within the school concerned. Where several teachers are involved in internally assessing the work of candidates, schools are encouraged to arrange to align their standards internally. Where *performing* is concerned, the main GCSE teacher, another class teacher, and a peripatetic teacher might well become involved in the process. Possibly the initial internal assessment would be made by the peripatetic teacher, then moderated by the GCSE class teacher. One of the aims of this initial stage of moderation is to establish a valid rank order of candidates before passing the moderation upwards to the Board concerned. The external moderation then runs on similar lines to those described for the NEA. Both composing and performing are moderated by a similar process.

NEA

As both *performing* and *composing* will be part of coursework, the moderation process for both components will be by inspection. With performing, a selection of recordings of performances from each Centre will be moderated, and the Moderator's assessment compared with the teacher's, with suggestions made for the adjustment of marks. The rank order of candidates determined by the teacher will not be altered. Moderators may visit Centres during the assessment process from time to time.

With *composing*, the Moderator will review a selection of folios/annotated tapes, on the same lines as for performing.

WJEC

Statistical moderation for *performing* – externally examined.

Moderation of *composing* will occur at three levels:

1 within Centres to ensure a reliable overall rank order;
2 through meetings organised on a regional basis;
3 through the inspection of samples of work from each Centre by the Group's Moderator.

NISEC

With *performing* being externally examined and therefore statistically moderated (on the whole), *composing* work will be moderated by inspection on lines similar to those described above. Teachers and moderators will be required to attend training sessions.

What kinds of grades are awarded for the GCSE?

GCSE grades will be awarded on a seven-point scale denoted by the letters A–G, and candidates who fail to achieve the minimum standards for Grade G will be awarded a 'U' or unclassified grade. The GCSE grades have an equivalent relationship with both O-level and CSE, which can be seen from the following table:

O-level	*GCSE*	*CSE*
A	A	
B	B	1 (GCSE A–C)
C	C	
D	D	2
E	E	3
	F	4
	G	5

There are two methods of grading: criterion-referenced, and norm-referenced. Norm-referencing is done on a statistical basis: a grade A may be awarded only to candidates whose marks fall in the top 5 per cent, the next 10 per cent are grade B, and so on. Criterion-referencing awards grades according to pre-determined standards, and each grade is defined in terms of the knowledge, skill and understanding that are to be shown by a candidate in order to qualify for a particular grade. Thus a candidate's grade depends on the quality of his or her work, and not on comparison with others.

CSE and O-level employed a system which was a mixture of criterion- and norm-referenced grading. GCSE, eventually, will operate a system which is entirely criterion-referenced. In order to do this, they will need to have a set of *Grade Criteria*, that is, a list of the skills and knowledge applicable for each grade. This system will need a great deal of fine-tuning, and until it can be put into operation (in the early 1990s, it is estimated) a selection of Grade Descriptions are provided in the National Criteria, and either repeated or expanded upon in the varying syllabuses.

In the composing component, the two Grade Descriptions given are as follows:

Examples of Grade F attainment

A typical Grade F candidate is likely to have shown the ability to present music in a basic form and be able to discuss it with the assessor if required. Compositions would demonstrate signs of technical knowledge and control of the medium used with design of ideas, e.g. a short march for trumpet, with a very simple rhythmic/harmonic accompaniment.

Examples of Grade C attainment

A typical Grade C candidate is likely to have shown the ability to present music in a finished form and be able to discuss it with the assessor if required. Compositions would demonstrate evidence of technical knowledge and control of the medium used with design and imaginative use of ideas and resources, e.g. a march for trumpet, synthesiser, piano and percussion with a contrasting middle section.

Until the establishment of Grade Criteria, such rough-and-ready guidelines will have to be used, and grading for GCSE will be a mixture of norm- and criterion-referencing as before.

Activity 28

Study the Grade Descriptions in your own syllabus (there may be some slight differences of emphasis or amplifications of those given in the Criteria), and make Grade Descriptions for what you estimate to be coursework attainments worthy of the remaining Grades (A, B, D, E and G). Write descriptions to cover prepared performing, unprepared performing and composing, using the standard wording given in the Criteria quoted above as your starting point.

Activity 29

Discuss a selection of pupils' taped and/or notated coursework with colleagues, with a view to coming to a consensus on grading. Use material from your own GCSE pupils if possible, supplemented by Examples from this book.

What points need to be borne in mind when communicating to pupils and parents?

The *Pocket Oxford Dictionary* defines 'musical', when applied to a person, as 'fond of, or skilled in, music'. This dual definition can be a cause of misunderstanding unless it is used carefully and explicitly by teachers. If parents are told that their child is 'musical' (without it being defined to what extent this means 'skilled in' or 'fond of' music) there could be considerable disillusion if the end-result turned out to be a grade lower than the word 'musical' had possibly led them to expect. Now that teachers themselves are the examiners where course-work is concerned, parents will rightly see them as being partially responsible for the grade obtained, and, by implication, for the pupil's future prospects.

With the move to criterion-referenced assessment, and with internal assessment playing such a large part in most GCSE schemes, the process of communicating to both pupils and parents about likely grade outcomes should become easier, and misinformation leading to disappointment can be avoided. The crucial stage of the link between the teacher and pupils and their families comes during the third year of secondary school, when subject selection for GCSE has to be made. By this time, feedback in the form of school reports and conversations, both at formal parents evenings and other more informal contacts, will have paved the way for a recommendation as to whether Music will be a rewarding and worthwhile subject to pursue, and also give an indication of the range of grades likely to be achieved by the pupil.

What type of pupil, then, is rewarded with high grades at GCSE? A pupil who can demonstrate 'all-round' musicianship, and also musicality on a number of levels, is more likely to achieve a high grade than one who demonstrates competence, or even excellence, at just one or two skills. Just as the Criteria demand that teachers be open to an 'enormous canvas', candidates who demonstrate a wide range of listening, performing and composing interests and skills will be rewarded. This is in marked contrast to the demands made on both teachers and pupils for O-level. So, a rock drummer may be technically excellent as a percussionist, and have the ability to drive along his band in an inspiring way, but if he shows neither interest nor aptitude in other aspects of the course, his brilliance at drumming and his effectiveness in ensemble will not, by themselves, be sufficient to guarantee him a high grade. However, such a pupil would not have been able to demonstrate his musical achievement at all at O-level, so the GCSE is a considerable advance in this respect. Given the wide ability-range catered for, and the other subject demands made on pupils at this age, we may well have a number of GCSE pupils whose keenness for music manifests itself through just one or two activities. A teacher must clarify to parents that a pupil will need to widen his or her musical vision in order to get the most out of the course. This problem of musicians (or artists generally) with expertise, often exceptional, in only one or two areas, is not confined to GCSE – many conservatoire students, especially singers, have been notoriously unable to cope with some of the more academic aspects of their courses.

One area in particular where lack of skill may penalise the pupil is that of staff notation. Although the Criteria state that pupils should be allowed to achieve, and have their achievements recognised, whether or not they are familiar with it, in reality one wonders how many pupils not conversant with the system will achieve Grades A or B? This is particularly applicable to the listening component, detailed discussion of which is outside the scope of this book. Nearly all the listening papers examined by the writer demand the ability to read staff notation. As the Criteria state:

> 1.4 It is acknowledged that staff notation must continue as a prime means of communication for music, although other forms of notation should not be excluded.

There has been a critical response in some quarters to what has been perceived as a narrow and limiting aspect of the Criteria. The ILEA Inspectorate in their paper 'GCSE Music, Which Syllabus?', state:

> This narrow view of relating sound to symbol will inhibit developments in those music departments in ILEA secondary schools which seek to incorporate a wide range of styles in their musical activities as advocated by the ILEA policies for Equal Opportunities. (p. 4)

Care and tact, therefore, is needed from the teacher in communicating both the extent and the nature of an individual's 'musicality' both to the pupil and to parents. One of the most useful forms of feedback is the school report, provided it is both subject-specific, and says rather more than the traditional 'one-liners' found in some schools. Terse and unhelpful phrases such as 'works well' will just not be sufficient any more. A more comprehensive document could read as follows:

> Alan is making good progress in his first term of GCSE Music. His skill on the clarinet, and his pass at Grade III should stand him in good stead for the performing part of the examination, and he is also a willing and useful member of the school wind band, which will help to prepare him for the ensemble performing part of the examination. He has composed two short pieces during this term, including a carefully thought out study for clarinet, which has some lively ideas, and shows a good understanding of what the instrument can do. He has some difficulty in notating his ideas in manuscript, but has recorded an effective performance onto tape.
>
> The weakest part of the examination work is his listening. Alan must try to listen more widely and more carefully. He is very interested in British traditional jazz, and has a good knowledge in this area, but he must broaden his range of musical interests to encompass other forms and styles.
>
> With his ability and accomplishment, Alan should obtain at least a Grade C in the GCSE, but with hard work and attention to one or two of the points noted above, he might achieve a Grade B or even an A. He certainly has the ability to do so.

The above, which picks out specific strengths and weaknesses, and makes a grade prediction, is a proper professional example of keeping both pupil and parents informed.

Activity 30

Make a sample course description for GCSE Music for parents, to be included in the papers circulated to them prior to a third year 'subject choice' parents' evening. Indicate the kind of skills and attitudes demanded of the new approach to the subject, especially the kind of homework and preparation needed for coursework. Many parents may be puzzled at the move away from what they will perceive as an 'academic' emphasis in the subject. Explain carefully why there will be less verbal written work, and more practical music-making.

Bibliography

Bunting, R. (1987) 'Composing Music: Case Studies in the Teaching and Learning Process', in *British Journal of Music Education*, Vol. 4, No. 1.

Department of Education and Science/Welsh Office (1985) *GCSE, a General Introduction*, London, HMSO.

Department of Education and Science/Welsh Office (1985) *GCSE General Criteria*, London, HMSO.

Department of Education and Science/Welsh Office (1985) *GCSE Music Criteria*, London, HMSO.

Department of Education and Science (1985) *Music from 5 to 16*, Curriculum Matters, 4, London, HMSO.

Gamble, T. (1978) quoted in 'Schools Council Project: Music in the Secondary School Curriculum' (1978).

Gamble, T. (1982) 'Outline of creative work for the first three years 1981–2', music syllabus reprinted in Paynter, J. (1982), pp. 187–99.

Gamble, T. (1984) 'Imagination and understanding in Music', in *British Journal of Music Education*, Vol. 1, No. 1, 7–25.

Inner London Education Authority (1978) *Music Guidelines*, London, ILEA.

Inner London Education Authority (1986) *GCSE Music: Which Syllabus?*, London, ILEA.

Inner London Education Authority (1986) *Sounds like mine – a normal activity*, a video programme about pupils composing, available from ILEA Learning & Resources, Television and Publishing Centre, Thackeray Road, London SW8 3JB.

Mobley, M., Emerson, C., Goddard, I. and Letch, R. (1986) *All about GCSE*, London, Heinemann.

Music Advisers' National Association (1986) *Assessment and progression in Music Education*, Music Advisers' National Association.

Newmarch, R. (ed.) (1906) *Life and Letters of Peter Ilich Tchaikowsky*, London, John Lane.

Orton, R. (1982) 'Assessment: a composer's view', in Paynter, J. (1982).

Orton, R. (1982) *Electronic music for schools*, Cambridge University Press.

Paynter, J. (1982) *Music in the Secondary School Curriculum*, Cambridge University Press.

Paynter, J. and Aston, P. (1970) *Sound and Silence*, Cambridge University Press.

Salaman, William (1984) *Living School Music*, Cambridge University Press.

Salaman, William (1986) 'GCSE – a Matter of Course', a series of articles in *Music Teacher*, Vol. 65, No. 3, pp. 9–13; No. 4, pp. 12–15; No. 5, pp. 9–13; No. 6, pp. 14–17.

Salaman, William (1987) *Composing and its assessment for GCSE*, WJEC, obtainable from the WJEC (address given at the end of this book).

Schools Council Project: Music in the Secondary School Curriculum (1978) *Music at Manland*, videotape programme, available from Drake Educational

Associates, 212 Whitchurch Road, Cardiff CF4 3XF.

Secondary Examinations Council (1985) *Coursework Assessment in GCSE*, Working Paper 2, London, SEC.

Secondary Examinations Council (1985) *Differentiated Assessment in GCSE*, Working Paper 1, London, SEC.

Secondary Examinations Council/Open University (1986) *GCSE, a Guide for Teachers*, the Open University Press.

Shapiro, N. and Hentoff, N. (1955) *Hear me talkin' to ya*, New York, Rinehart.

Spencer, P. (1980) 'The Blues, a practical project for the classroom' and 'The creative possibilities of pop', in Vulliamy and Lee (eds).

Stein, E. (1962) *Form and Performance*, London, Faber.

Steinitz, P. (1963) *Harmony and Counterpoint with the Masters*, London, Novello.

Stravinsky, I. and Craft, R. (1962) *Expositions and Developments*, London, Faber.

Swanwick, K. (1979) *A Basis for Music Education*, Windsor, NFER.

Vulliamy, G. and Lee, E. (eds) (1980) *Pop Music in School*, second edition, Cambridge University Press.

Vulliamy, G. and Lee, E. (eds) (1982) *Pop, Rock, and Ethnic Music in School*, Cambridge University Press.

Contents of tape

Side 1

Performing

1 Solo performance

(a) Study in D by Heller for piano, interpretations by two different pupils.
(b) Hymn tune, 'All creatures of our God and King' played on the trombone.
(c) 'Trumpet tune' by Purcell, two performances, played by the same pupil on cornet.
(d) Slow movement of 'cello sonata by Willem de Fesch, with piano accompaniment.
(e) Chopin, Prelude in C minor for piano.

2 Group performance

(a) Theme tune from the Largo of Dvorák's *New World* symphony. (Lower-school class group).
(b) 'Dido's Lament' by Purcell, performed in an *ad hoc* arrangement by oboe, saxophone, piano and bass guitar.
(c) Group performance (two performers), improvisation over a simple repeated chord progression. Drummer, accompanied by keyboard player, reggae style. Two takes.
(d) Irish–American folk song, 'Stewball', performed by two girls.

3 Improvisations on the 12-bar blues

(a) Bass xylophone solo (two 'takes').
(b) Vocal blues (two 'choruses' from the same 'take').
(c) A piano boogie-woogie, three choruses.
(d) A blues for solo guitar, three choruses.

Composing

4 Group compositions by lower-school pupils

(a) Melody in ABABA form for glockenspiel and metallophone.
(b) A piece for recorders and pitched percussion.
(c) Two pieces exploring (i) a cymbal, and (ii) an old piano frame.

5 Examples of 'head arrangements'

(a) 'Michael row the boat ashore'.
(b) 'Swing low', three arrangements: (i) for three xylophones, (ii) for three xylophones and bongoes, (iii) for voice, drums and bongoes.
(c) 'God rest you merry, gentlemen', for voice and piano.

Side 2

6 A piano duet

7 Two pieces by the same pupil

(a) Rondo for solo flute.
(b) Rondo for flute and bassoon.

8 A duet for flute and clarinet

9 Three piano pieces

(a) 'Sunrise'.
(a) 'A prelude'.
(c) 'Infinity'.

10 Two songs

(a) 'I was wrong'.
(b) 'The Schoolboy'.

GCSE Examining Groups

Note: All references to syllabuses in this booklet concern the 1988 examinations.

London and East Anglian Group (LEAG)

East Anglian Examinations Board, The Lindens, Lexden Road, Colchester, CO3 3RL (Tel. 0206 549595).

London Regional Examining Board, Lyon House, 104 Wandsworth High Street, London SW18 4LF (Tel. 01 870 2144).

University of London School Examinations Board, Stewart House, 32 Russell Square, London WC1 5DP (Tel. 01 636 8000).

Southern Examining Group (SEG)

Associated Examining Board, Stag Hill House, Guildford, Surrey, GU2 5XJ (Tel. 0483 506506).

South East Regional Examinations Board, 2–10 Mount Ephraim Road, Tunbridge Wells, Kent TN1 1EU (Tel. 0892 35311/2/3/4).

Southern Regional Examination Board, Avondale House, 33 Carlton Crescent, Southampton SO9 4YL (Tel. 0703 32312).

The South Western Examinations Board, 23–29 Marsh Street, Bristol BS1 4BP (Tel. 0272 273434).

University of Oxford Delegacy of Local Examinations, Ewert Place, Banbury Road, Summertown, Oxford OX7 7BZ (Tel. 0865 54291).

Midland Examining Group (MEG)

East Midland Examinations Board, Robins Wood House, Robins Wood Road, Aspley, Nottingham NG8 3NR (Tel. 0602 296021).

Oxford and Cambridge Schools Examinations Board, 10 Trumpington Street, Cambridge, CB2 1QB (Tel. 0223 64326).

Oxford and Cambridge Schools Examinations Board, Elsfield Way, Oxford, OX2 8EP (Tel. 0865 54421).

Southern Universities Joint Board, Cotham Road, Cotham, Bristol, BS6 6DD (Tel. 0272 736042).

The West Midlands Examinations Board, Norfolk House, Smallbrook, Queensway, Birmingham B5 4NJ (Tel. 021 643 2081).

University of Cambridge Local Examinations Syndicate, Syndicate Buildings, 1 Hills Road, Cambridge CB1 2EU (Tel. 0223 61111).

Northern Examining Association (NEA)

Associated Lancashire Schools Examining Board, 12 Harter Street, Manchester, M1 6HL (Tel. 061 228 0084).

Joint Matriculation Board, Manchester, M15 6EU (Tel. 061 273 2565).

Northern Regional Examinations Board, Wheatfield Road, Westerhope, Newcastle upon Tyne, NE5 5JZ (Tel. 091 286 2711).

North West Regional Examinations Board, Orbit House, Albert Street, Eccles, Manchester, M30 0WL (Tel. 061 788 9521).

Yorkshire and Humberside Regional Examinations Board, 31–33 Springfield Avenue, Harrogate, North Yorkshire, HG1 2HW (Tel. 0423 66991).

Yorkshire and Humberside Regional Examinations Board, Scarsdale House, 136 Derbyshire Lane, Sheffield, S8 8SE, (Tel. 0742 557436).

Welsh Joint Education Committee (WJEC)

Welsh Joint Education Committee, 245 Western Avenue, Cardiff CF5 2YX (Tel. 0222 561231).

Northern Ireland Schools Examination Council (NISEC)

Northern Ireland Schools Examination Council, Beechill House, 42 Beechill Road, Belfast, BT8 4RS (Tel. 0232 704666).